HOW TO DEVELOP
YOUR SPIRITUALITY
Volume 1

ALSO BY MASAHISA GOI

MASAHISA GOI

HOW TO DEVELOP
your spirituality

Volume 1

Copyright © 2014 Masahisa Goi
All rights reserved.

ISBN-13: 978-1-4992-3853-2
ISBN-10: 1-4992-3853-3

Originally published in Japanese as chapters 1-7 of
霊性の開発 (*Reisei no kaihatsu*), Byakko Press, 1961.

Publisher: Masato Hiramoto.
Senior Editor: Mary L. McQuaid.
Cooperating Editor: David W. Edelstein.
Translated from the Japanese by Kinuko Hamaya and Mary McQuaid.
Contributing Translators: Brandon Kurohara and Grace Roberts.

Designed by David W. Edelstein.
Cover image: Fotolia.com
Title page illustration: HyuuggaHinata on DeviantArt.com

CONTENTS

PREFACE

Even the desire for my own happiness
Melts into my prayer of dawn and dusk
For peace on earth

For a long time, I have been thinking and thinking about just one thing. I earnestly wanted to find a way for each person to be truly happy, and for our individual happiness to be perfectly merged with the happiness of all humanity at the same time.

If you truly love others, you cannot enjoy your own happiness when you see that many other people are unhappy. At the same time, if you want to give up all your own personal concerns and devote yourself entirely to working for the happiness of humanity, you need to have an unusually resilient and lofty character to carry it out.

There are people who have sought to perfect their own existence by following a spiritual path, but I do not believe they have been able to do so without thinking about the peace of the world at the same time. When the desire for self-perfection departs from humanitarian love, it can no longer be called self-perfection. Rather, it has slipped into mere self-gratification. That is why I feel that if you are seeking truth, self-perfection must go hand in hand with humanitarian love.

Realistically speaking, most of us find that we have our hands full just trying to feed ourselves and our families, and it is no easy matter for us to steadily devote ourselves to self-perfection. On top of that, how inexpressibly difficult it would be to try and work for the good of society as well! This is something that pains the hearts of conscientious people and deepens their anxieties even further.

This collection of essays was created for conscientious people like this, and it is also meant to reconcile the minds of the masses of people on earth who are still, for the most part, hoping to catch hold of whatever worldly benefits they can. Although the method it proposes is an easy one to practice, it is also a worthy one, and is explained from various angles.

Even if it may be easy to practice, unless a teaching resonates with a high and pure vibration, it cannot satisfy the intellects of responsible and conscientious people. In creating this method, from start to finish, my intention was to faithfully reflect the divine mind, without clashing with humanity's day to day way of living. What emerged was the method of prayer for world peace—a practice that enlightens the individual and humanity as a whole, both at the same time. A large number of people have already concurred with this method and made it their own.

It is my hope that those who read this book will naturally appreciate the profound meaning of the poem at the start of this preface. I have no doubt that the divine principle it conveys—that our own spiritual development is naturally linked with the happiness of humanity as a whole—will strike a chord in your heart.

Masahisa Goi
January 1961

FREEDOM OF MIND

Human beings long for freedom. In all societies, throughout the ages, people have wanted to live their lives in the way they wish.

There are two kinds of freedom—outer freedom and inner freedom. The former is freedom from external constraints, while the latter is freedom from internal constraints and attachments. Usually, though, people think only of the external kind. They see 'freedom' simply as the absence of external restraints. They generally equate it with giving free rein to the ego and making things go the way they want them to. Most people never think about inner freedom.

This way of thinking has gone on since ancient times. When their desire for outer freedom has gone unsatisfied, people have tended to give up, driving themselves down into a state of hopeless resignation.

In post-war Japan, there were some who felt energized

11

by the world 'liberalism.' In trying to attain greater outer freedom (the freedom to satisfy the ego), many of them ended up trampling on the freedom of others and assailing people's inner, human dignity. In doing so, they became more and more attached to their own egocentric desires, deepening them even further. As a result, they provoked social confusion, and dragged down their inner human divinity, which is true freedom itself. To act in this way is to act without knowing the true nature of freedom. This misconception of freedom is a fearful thing for humankind.

Even if all your external restraints were removed, you could not say that you had attained true freedom. There are people and nations who insist that the present capitalistic systems are bad, and that only the systems of socialism and communism can liberate humankind. But in truth, no reformation of a social system can really free people and let them experience a truly happy life.

No system or ideology will ever bring people freedom if its concept of freedom or happiness covers external movements alone. This is because such a view of freedom or happiness is rooted in outward appearances. It is not the freedom or happiness that wells out of the inner self— the true, divine self.

The things provided by the external world are constantly shifting and changing. For as long as the leaders who take control of the external world, and those working under them, are motivated by materially-oriented desires, and live by the emotions connected with the five senses, all social and political policies are sure to go on changing along with the daily movements of those people's emotions.

The freedom of everyone who comes under the influence of those leaders is outwardly affected by those shifts and changes. Of course, it goes without saying that the changes are totally beyond the control of the average person, since the leaders could not carry out any policy if they had to ask for agreement from each individual affected by it.

As a result, only a small number of people in leading positions can make and carry out policies, enjoying their own outer freedom. Meanwhile, the freedom of the general population is continually suppressed. But even the freedom of the leaders is fragile and superficial. No one can say how long it will last; it could collapse at any moment. And so, in order to preserve their outer 'freedom,' their thoughts are filled with plots and schemes that cover the brightness of their inner selves, and their minds cannot afford even a day's rest.

In this situation, both the leaders and the general population are defining 'freedom' and 'happiness' only in terms of the external world. Even if their aims concern the nation or humanity, their policies and actions are always caught up in the flow of shifting thought waves. This is why they can have no stability at all.

When we look at it this way, it becomes clear that true freedom and happiness cannot be found through external policies of any kind. They well up from within us. Freedom and happiness can be attained only from the inner self—the true self.

What is a human being?

We must now consider the question *What is a human being?* or *What am I?* Without knowing the answer to this, you can never find true freedom, nor can you let your mind soar freely, without restriction.

A human being is neither flesh nor thoughts. Our physical body is our container—our workplace. Our thoughts are a current of light waves that we emit. Or, they could also be a flow of karmic waves—in other words, light mixed with darkness.

As long as our true mind is covered by karmic thought waves relating to our physical attachments and desires, we human beings cannot bring out our true divinity. We cannot reach a free and open state of mind.

There is never a moment when human beings are separated from the infinite source of their life. There is not a single person who is not connected to a flow of light from the one great life known as 'God.'

Everything, be it wisdom, wealth, or power, is within the one, great life. Yet, most people today do not even realize that they are connected to any great life. Or, even if they know it in theory, they do not believe it or let it show through in their actions. They are madly rushing about, seeking wisdom, wealth, and power from a different kind of world. I wonder where they could hope to find a world outside the realm of the absolute source of all life (God).

Thoughts that are out of tune with that original world are thoughts of illusion, darkness, or karma. Karmic thoughts were first produced after human beings descended to the physical world and became accustomed to living there. (When I say 'descended,' I mean that spiritual bodies descended from other heavenly spheres and slowed down their vibrations, forming the subconscious body, then the physical body, and began to inhabit the earthly world.) As they gradually forgot about their native home in a higher dimensional world, they concentrated on using earthly power to acquire knowledge, strength, and riches. This kind of materially-oriented thinking has continued up to the present, and nowadays it has become commonly accepted to think that there are no human worlds other than the physical one.

Since this way of thinking is the basis of all political policies and all social behavior today, the formation of a true world of peace and happiness has, of course, not yet been completed.

However hard people might try to use wisdom in their karmic thinking, and however comfortable and well-ordered their external life might be, this can never bring them close to true happiness or a truly harmonious world. Karmic thinking always limits people to a physically-oriented lifestyle. It makes people seek happiness in physical terms alone. This is why karmic thinking always ends up making people defend themselves and suppress others for the sake of their own physical welfare. It can never bring people together in a happy, harmonious way of living.

Relativistic thinking never unifies people. We can never have a sense of oneness with others if we think that our existence is separate from theirs. To become one with others, we must first shake off the notion that we are nothing but our physical body. We must change and expand our way of thinking to see ourselves as life itself, connected with the one, great life.

If we existed apart from others, and if our interests ran counter to theirs, there would be no reason for us to experience unity with them or to share enjoyment with them. This can be said about individuals and also about nations. Unless people rid themselves of karmic thinking—which comes from the idea of separateness—I do not believe that true peace and harmony can ever be hoped for, no matter how far civilization might advance.

Let us think about this in terms of just one family: parents and children, husband and wife, brothers and sisters. Physically, each of them exists separately from the others. Yet when they live in harmony, each helping the others, they are naturally aware of their shared home, heritage, and common interests. On the other hand, when each person is preoccupied only with his or her own interests and emotions, harmony is lost and the family is plunged into situations of conflict and resentment.

The belief that oneself and others are separate entities is a mistaken type of individualism, called 'egoism.' For as long as people hold this view, their lives will always be in turmoil. Emotional turmoil arises from not knowing the true identity of human beings, and from not knowing the love that is the essence of each one of us. For people in this situation, there is no way to experience freedom of mind.

To have freedom of mind is to really know the true and original substance of a human being. It is to constantly attune our thoughts to our true self (God). When we have a free and open mind, we do not fix our attention on the karmic occurrences of happiness or unhappiness, gain or loss, that are continually flowing in front of us. We can recognize these shifting things as the shadows of our own mistaken thoughts from the past, making their appearance in the process of fading away. Even if we do catch hold of those karmic waves, we can quickly release them and return our thoughts to our true self.

The missions of religion and science

It is already out of date to think of a human being as a fixed, limited body, or of matter as a concrete, tangible form. We are in a modern age, when atomic power is beginning to be put to practical use. It is now being discovered that all matter is the assemblage of invisibly minute atoms. Naturally, this also applies to the physical human body.

Scientists have also discovered that an atom has a nucleus at its center, containing protons and neutrons. The nucleus is surrounded by electrons circuiting around it. They have also identified a number of mesons, and say that there are many other undetected particles whose functions are vital to an atom.

It is yet to be discovered how and why these particles function. In an interview with a Tokyo newspaper, the *Yomiuri Shimbun*, the prominent physicist Dr. Hideki Yukawa has commented:

In addition to these discoveries, we have found many things that mystify us. We know next to nothing about the essence of the world in which we live. To behave as if we knew everything would be a very careless attitude.

These are the words of a true scientist. To honestly state that they do not understand something, and from there to advance theories and conduct experiments, step by step, is the approach taken by fine and worthy scientists.

Unfortunately, though, the attitudes of some heedless scholars and intellectuals are quite unscientific, even though they voice the word 'science' very often. They have a bad habit of denying or sneering at things that surpass the limits of their knowledge and experience, saying that those things do not exist or calling them 'superstitions.'

The role of science is to analyze the tangible world, with academic and technological assistance, in a quest for the essence of the human world and the origin of the universal system. Any scientific advance, large or small, is a step toward that goal. Science explores the secrets of the world of Mu^1 (無) or Kuu^2 (空), starting from the world of outward appearances. Its aim is to clarify and explain, without any mystification. Thus, science advances as each of its branches continues to build and expand its own framework of study.

Science holds an important key for the progress of human culture and civilization. However, up to now its contributions have been limited to the external world, the world of materials. It has done little to develop the internal world, the world of the mind. As a result, the responsibility for a human being's inner (spiritual) development has been left up to people of religion. They, by and large, have focused their efforts on fostering mental calmness and stability.

In contrast to scientists, who investigate the tangible world with the aid of machines and instruments, people of religion directly seek what is invisible and intangible to the physical eyes and hands: the mind. Setting aside material considerations, their method is to focus their attention on the original self, the divine, the source of life. In other words, they believe from the start in the mysterious, absolute power and wisdom that operates the universe, and they strive to be one with it by concentrating their thoughts on it.

Once we become one with that power, the mysteries of humankind and the universe naturally become clear to us. This is because the absolute being, the creator of the universe, is the parent of everything, and would naturally know everything about the offspring that it gave birth to.

Sakyamuni Buddha and Jesus Christ are recognized as being among those who came closest to this perfect state of mind, which can be called 'freedom of mind.'

Our thought waves create an atmosphere around us

When we leave behind our selfish desires, our true mind comes to reflect itself in our daily words and actions. Since our true self is a radiant light, rooted in the divine, our words, actions, and lifestyle begin to shine. Because this radiant light is in a different category from that of the material world, its brilliance is not clearly perceived by most people, but I do think they can feel a brightness, gentleness, and warmth without knowing exactly what it is. As we approach this state, we give others a pleasant sensation of pureness, clearness, and brightness.

Leaving behind selfish desires can also be described as thinking about and working for others, thinking about and working for society, and thinking about and working for humankind and the earth. In short, it is to do only works of love. When our true self appears on the surface, it means that God is manifested there. God is all of everything, and God is Love. Thus, when the divine mind moves in us, we are actively sending out thoughts and actions of love.

The further removed we are from selfish desires, the fewer attachments we have, and the more we call forth our true freedom of mind. This new self, when seen through spiritual eyes, seems to radiate light.

People with psychic perceptions have a particular sensitivity for discerning fine, spiritual vibrations that are undetectable to physical eyes. This is similar to the way scientists discovered atoms by using certain instruments. Our thoughts are invisible to physical eyes, but they swirl and flow out around us, forming various shapes. The accumulation of these thoughts over a long period of time, extending far back through previous lifetimes, creates an atmosphere that affects others. At the same time, it constructs the various circumstances we encounter and the course of our future life. This atmosphere, to the eyes of a person with psychic perceptions, is seen either as light or as a dark cloud.

The most important moment in the improvement of your fate

When such people see those thought waves, they perceive the height of our spirituality and the nature of our daily actions. The soul of a person who always lives with humanitarian love is shining. Being a deeply loving person is, in itself, evidence that our true self is being expressed. In other words, it proves that our divine self is actively working.

The nobleness or baseness of our character is clearly shown in our thought waves. However, since a machine that distinguishes those thought waves has not yet been invented, only a small number of psychic people can perceive them.

Now, let us set aside the thoughts of others and make it our first priority to nurture the fine quality of our own personality, and to create the right future life for us. In order to do this, first and foremost, we must attune our thinking to the divine—the world of light, love, and thoughtfulness.

You may have had thoughts of surpassing others, or found diversion in finding ways to entrap others. You may have hated others and hurt others. But since those thoughts are far from the divine, far from the light, they produce a dark cloud around you, covering your inner light with dark waves. To the extent that your inner light is covered, you have distanced yourself from true happiness and true freedom.

When this dark cloud made up of negative thought

waves fully envelops you, it spontaneously ruptures. This brings about some sort of catastrophe in your life, or causes your life to take a sudden turn for the worse. In the distress of such a time, consciously or unconsciously, you always reflect upon and reconsider your past behavior.

Since those negative thoughts and actions come not only from your present lifetime, but also from previous lifetimes, misfortunes can happen even if you are not thinking about or doing anything bad now. In other words, when misfortune or catastrophe occurs, it definitely means that your past errors are revealing themselves in the external world now, at the time when they are meant to disappear.

The moment when your past negative thoughts and actions disappear is the most important moment in the improvement of your fate. If you do not know this, you might blame heaven, vilify others, cry over your miserable situation, and lose courage.

Do not attach your thoughts to good or to bad

In order to live brightly, courageously and strongly, always facing a better and better future, it is important to believe in God and believe in divine love. At the same time, firmly believe that your miseries and misfortunes are the repayments of your debts from the past, and that after they have disappeared, divine love and power will surely manifest themselves in you.

If you have recognized your error, a momentary reflection will suffice; you do not need to blame yourself for it over and over again. Because it was something un-harmonious, it emerged in your life in order to fade away and vanish. Any misfortune that has come to you so far has disappeared already, so there is no need to worry over it any longer. The important thing is to put your thoughts in good order, and stay firmly connected with your true self, with the help of your divine and spiritual protec-tors.[3] Keep asking them to guide you in accomplishing your missions. If you do this while moving straight ahead with your life, you can be sure that a good future will open up for you.

If you entertain too much regret over your mistakes, this will smother your courage. Your thoughts will en-trench themselves in gloom, casting a dank cloud over the radiant, inner light that is meant to shine. Do not attach your thoughts either to good or to bad. Know that, in the beginning, your limited self did not exist. Good and bad are the intersections of light and shadow that form only in the process of projecting the true images of divinity here on earth. Thoughts adhering to good or bad obstruct the flow of life, causing it to waver and distort into karma. This delays the construction of the divine world here on earth.

The 'good' and 'bad' of this relative world of shapes and forms will eventually disappear. After that, the world of light that transcends the relativity of 'good' and 'bad' will manifest itself. In that divine realm, everyone lives only in mutual good will. This is why I am urging peo-ple to do their utmost to free their thoughts from such attachments.

Return to your original self

In the Bible it is written: *In the beginning was the Word, and the Word was with God, and the Word was God.* (John 1:1)

Originally, everything was in God. However, after the formation of the physical world, people began to think that the divine and physical worlds were separate. They stopped thinking about the divine world altogether, regarding the physical world as the only true existence. That mistaken way of thinking, born from ignorance and darkness, is at the source of all of humanity's miseries. It is important to quiet your mind and give serious thought to this.

Sakyamuni Buddha became aware of this, and so he taught people that everything exists in *Kuu* (emptiness). He taught them to once and for all reject the existence of the external, phenomenal world, severing themselves from all the thoughts and desires connected with it.

What most human beings think of as 'themselves' is actually their daily, habitual thoughts. They regard their life only as something contained within the limited physical body. But this is not the true scope of our life.

Think about the sea. The waves on the sea are not the sea itself. If we looked only at the waves, thinking that they are all there is to the sea, it wouldn't be right, would it? Our thoughts are the waves, and our life is the sea.

As soon as possible, we human beings need to overturn the fallacy that life is confined to the physical body, and that 'thoughts' are the same as mind. Until we rise above this huge misunderstanding, we will be unable to transform this human world into a world of truth and harmony.

Everyone, quiet your thoughts. Closely observe your inner selves. Intently call to the guardian divinities and spirits who exist within you and around you. Continuously ask them to guide you in illuminating your true self. If you do, you will attain freedom of mind. This is my urgent message to everyone in the world.

Your guardian spirits are always just above your head, with your guardian divinity (angel) even higher above. With their light waves, they have been steadily doing their utmost to purify the mistaken thought waves that you have been emitting since ages past. They are doing this to help you uncover your true, divine self. If you continue to thank your divine and spiritual guardians, you will surely attain a keen awareness of their existence.

FOCUS ON THE REAL YOU

Though human beings live amid mysteries that are beyond their limited human understanding, many people have become so accustomed to these mysteries that they live their lives without feeling the wonder or mystery of them at all. Birth, growth, being able to think; such miracles as water, air and food; the fact that everything needed to sustain human life is naturally provided—there is no end to the list of wonders which occur on our planet. However, not only do some people have no reverence for the mysteries of life and the universe, they even deny the very existence of those mysteries. They think that they can live solely by means of their own, individual power, and bring happiness to humanity with that power alone. Sometimes I think about these people and marvel at the strangeness of their thinking, which, I must confess, strikes me as being altogether absurd.

If a feeling of reverence and thankfulness for everything

around us that enables us to live does not well up in our hearts, what means could we possibly have of attaining true happiness? If someone is not yet aware that our physical bodies are able to live because we are given our life-power from a source that is within us and around us, they have not taken the first step forward on the road to truth. Knowing the truth is out of the question for people who cannot feel true gratitude toward that mysterious power.

How can there be people who, when faced with the source of the mysterious power that causes everything in the universe to function and works actively within the physical body of every individual human being, deny this existence or hesitate to call it God? To me, this is a mystery indeed.

Until the mysteries of the power known as 'life,' which activates human beings and controls our every bodily function, are fully understood and explained, any scientist has to acknowledge that the question of life is still a mystery, and treat it with reverence. Surely they cannot deny that the source of those mysteries is a power beyond that of the physical body.

I say this because, with the phenomenon called 'death,' the mysterious power called 'life' leaves the physical body. Even though the body continues to exist, without life it becomes nothing more than a material substance with no ability to function. Where does the power called 'life' hide itself after death? Until we can locate it precisely, there is no alternative but to treat life as a mystery.

Where does life come from and where does it go? When I observe people neglecting this profound issue and dismissing with a laugh concepts such as 'mystery' or 'God,' I can only find them childish and dogmatic. If people who have such arrogant attitudes and philosophies as to repudiate the existence of God and all that is mysterious play a central role in running their country and the world, what kind of future do you suppose the planet Earth will have?

The deluded businessman

Atheists and other materially-minded people say that the only things that exist are those that can be seen with the eyes, felt with the hands, or otherwise perceived through the five senses. According to them, such things as wisdom and the emotions are supplementary functions which begin to occur at birth and develop along with the physical body. Likewise, they maintain that the physical body is all there is to a human being.

They try to develop their 'physical' wisdom and knowledge in order to search the universe for materials that will make the world we live in as comfortable as possible. In these efforts, they completely overlook the reality that the earth and indeed the universe offer living environments to human beings, or that the union of the two sexes produces an embryo, which will be born as a baby and will continue to grow. They try to completely ignore God—the great power that holds infinite wisdom, abundance, and ability, and bestows all sorts of blessing upon human beings.

This is like the situation of a businessman who starts a company with everything he needs—including buildings, staff, and goods—being provided by investors. However, once he starts the business, the businessman completely forgets about the existence of the investors, their capital, and their various other favors. He not only neglects to pay them dividends, but even ignores their existence, and lives under the illusion that all the business has ever needed are the people who are actively involved in its operation.

This deluded businessman is in the same condition in which atheists and materialists find themselves. As far as they are concerned, life is a kind of material resource that exists separately within each physical body and serves as its individual power supply. They never give a thought to the interchange of life among people, animals, and plants, because their routine method is to deny everything that is not visible or detectable by conventional instruments.

The error of rejecting divinity

Because materially-minded people do not even try to think about what to spiritually-minded people is such a plainly evident truth—that life is allotted to each individual from the invisible divine world, and that it is shared among people—their view on life is so short-sighted as to think it is confined to a physical form. They think that if this form, the physical body, perishes, the life in it perishes as well.

When people give no thought to what they are before their birth or after death, and do not recognize the divine life-energy that is eternally at work within a human being—through his or her subconscious, spiritual, and divine aspects—it is not surprising that they have little reverence or respect for their own life or the lives of others. This is why hurting others for their own benefit, or for the sake of their own groups and organizations, does not bring any pain to their hearts at all.

Since materialists do not recognize that they are spirits branching out from the unlimited source of life, they tend not to feel gratitude for their life or the lives of others, to say nothing of being grateful to God and everything around them. It is a pity for them that they cannot experience the true pleasure that springs from such gratitude, and there is no end to their complaints and their dissatisfaction. Likewise, because they utterly neglect to understand the reason for human life and the true role of humanity, they justify everything to the advantage of their own groups. Carried along by the flow of their karmic thoughts, they chase after their own selfish goals using means fair or foul, regardless of the troubles that other people or other groups might suffer.

The views on world unification and peace held by people who are feckless enough to reject what is divine or mysterious, who have no understanding of what happened when humans first appeared on earth, and who have not resolved the mysteries of a human being's inner systems, are, to the eyes of divine beings, very shallow and can only drive humanity into even deeper suffering. From my own experience, I can say with certainty that human beings are divine spirits who are working to manifest our divine identity on the earthly plane. Because I have experienced the human existence in the spiritual and subconscious worlds (refer to the subsection *My own experience* below), however ardently those who repudiate divinity and the existence of any human worlds other than the physical one may claim to know the way to world peace and the happiness of humanity, I can firmly declare that they are mistaken.

A way of thinking that rejects what is divine can hold no reverence for life and allows for no exchange of love, which derives from a feeling of oneness with others. This is because true love is itself a manifestation of divinity. The mysterious being—that great, all-inclusive divine life—has apportioned itself into various distinct lives, and works within each individual human spirit. When those spirits, or divisions of God, melt into oneness with one another, the vibration or reverberation that we know as love is produced.

No one can live, even for a moment, without receiving light from his or her divine source—not even materialists or atheists are exempt from this principle.

Why do people reject divinity?

When we are receiving all these wonderful gifts from our divine source, how can there still be people who reject its existence or lose their sense of gratitude? It is because the waves of humanity's selfish desires, accumulated over many lifetimes, have completely covered up the divine spirits, or light, within them, in the same way a dark cloud covers the moonlight. Although their divine light still shines inside, waves of karmic thoughts form a deep and thick cover that prevents the effect of that light from being felt in their external thoughts and actions. Such people reject the existence of God because they are completely unable to sense God functioning, and so with others like them they swim about in karmic waves of selfish desires, which stem from their attachment to the preservation of their own physical bodies. When they die, they usually fall into the world of their thoughts, the subconscious world, or the state of mind that is called 'hell'—a realm of relentless distress, bereft of God, light, and love. There, they suffer all sorts of self-inflicted anguish until they become humble enough to recognize that their lives are indeed part of that divine source, and that it is because of the divine source of life that they are able to live.

Since God is the great parent in which a human being's true mind resides, it should be clear how ignorant and rash it is to live without thinking of that divine parent. It is important for us to always desire and strive for our thoughts to be one with God—our own original self.

In the beginning, if you cannot think of God, you could start by giving thanks to everything around you that enables you to live. Air, water, food, the earth, the sun, parents, family, friends—all these enable us to live, to grow, and to feel strengthened. Therefore, it is only natural for us to feel thankful to them. When we do this, we are unconsciously acknowledging divine love. At this stage, we do not necessarily have to call upon God. Sooner or later, though, it will become necessary to advance one step further and study in depth the relationship between us and the origin of our life. Otherwise, we will never be able to recognize the truth of human beings. And without knowing the truth of human beings, we cannot live our lives with any sense of stability and confidence.

My own experience

I have clearly learned from my own experience that, in addition to the physical world, there are the following worlds: the subconscious world, where my thoughts once existed; the spiritual world, a world even finer and higher than the subconscious world, where I also existed; and the divine world, where my divine self lived firmly and vividly. (This experience is more fully described in my book, *One Who Unites Heaven and Earth.*[4]) I experienced how human beings, while existing as physical beings, simultaneously exist in the subconscious, spiritual, and divine worlds. In other words, a human being's subconscious, spiritual, and divine selves exist simultaneously in the vessel called the physical body. It may be more precise to say that I was led to that experience by my guardian divinity, who has been protecting me since before I was born. Immediately after that experience, I began to devote myself entirely to my work as an independent spiritual leader, having confirmed my existence in the divine world while I still possessed my physical body.

What I have been teaching people is based on this experience. A human being is, in reality, a divine existence, and is light itself. At our divine source, everything is one light. This light is divided out into rays, each of which fulfills a particular function. A single ray uses an individual physical body to work from. Therefore, it is a mistake to assume that the physical body is all there is to a human being. Since the physical body is a vessel and is the field of activity for a human being's life, or true self, we must always purify the various desires that arise in connection with it. If we limit ourselves to the physical body, assuming that it is all there is to our lives, those erroneous thoughts, and the selfish desires that are removed from God, obstruct the truth of human beings: that we are God in the divine world, spirit in the spiritual world, and soul in the subconscious world. This obstruction prevents the truth from functioning in the physical world in the form of light vibrations. As long as we limit ourselves in this way, we can never improve the course of our lives or bring happiness to humanity.

Keep thinking of the real you

I clearly distinguish the real person, or true self, from karmic thoughts of exultation, anger, sorrow, pleasure, sexual desire, jealousy, and so on, and I have been teaching people accordingly: The true human being, or true self, is God itself and light itself, and it is immortal. On the other hand, karmic thought waves vanish as soon as they appear. Knowing this, the best thing to do would be to continue summoning your true self in your heart. Whenever something that you find irritating or troublesome occurs, do not attach yourself to it, but direct your thoughts to your divine self, and understand that karmic thought waves from your past, including your previous lifetimes, have just appeared and immediately vanished away. At the same time, do not neglect, even for a moment, to thank your guardian spirits (your spiritual ancestors who have reached their awakening) and your guardian divinity, the divine being up above your guardian spirits. These divine and spiritual protectors are working ceaselessly on your behalf to guide you toward a bright future.

When even ten percent of humanity raise the level of their thinking to bring it in accord with their true mind, and work diligently while remaining faithful to the light of their true mind, the unharmonious thought waves in this world will be purified at once, and a peaceful and bright world—a world free of hatred and conflict—will be born.

Therefore, it is vital to stop blaming yourself and other people for all the mistakes and wrongdoings, and to forgive one another, knowing that those actions are the vanishing shadows of the whole world's illusory thoughts, most of them carried over from past lifetimes. Moreover, it will help enormously if you keep a grateful heart and ask for all people's guardian divinities and spirits to let that karma disappear as quickly as possible. I consider this to be of the utmost importance.

As long as you continue to chase after your own and other people's mistakes, a happy world will never take shape. This is because you are shrouded in waves of karmic thoughts, and have lost sight of the real you—your real, divine self.

Whatever kind of karma appears in whatever kind of situation, it vanishes away if you keep a steady mind, without allowing your thoughts to move. You do not have to struggle with the karma that appears, or try to force it away. All you need to do is quietly ask for the protection of your guardian divinity and guardian spirits, and any evil or misery will absolutely vanish. It is crucial for you to know this and believe in it.

I have been encouraging people to believe first of all in the love of God, secondly that they are spirits from God, and thirdly that karmic thoughts definitely vanish with the passage of time.

Evils are bound to vanish. Miseries are bound to vanish. Any and all greedy and selfish thoughts are bound to vanish if you continue to think of God. I myself have experienced this to be the truth.

Karma moves in rapid cycles

Karmic thought waves move in tremendously rapid cycles in the human worlds (physical and subconscious), as well as in each individual's physical and subconscious embodiments, and it is therefore very difficult indeed to extract ourselves completely from those cycles solely by means of our own physical power in the physical world.

The cycle of movement from the subconscious body (commonly called 'the subconscious') to the physical body (conscious state), and back is so violent that if a thought that has been hidden in the subconscious body comes in to contact with a similar thought from another person, or with some sort of incident, it suddenly reveals itself, giving rise to such emotions as anger, sadness, jealousy, arrogance, desire, and malicious feelings towards others. The force of these emotions is so unbridled that, even if we try to restrain them, they still appear in our thoughts and actions. Even if we have managed to restrain them by sheer force of will, it does not mean that these emotions have been extinguished. They have merely been suppressed and squeezed back into the subconscious. Eventually, they will emerge again many times stronger in the words and actions of the physical body. If we continue to restrain them, those karmic thoughts will emerge later in the form of misfortune, illness, or failure.

While it is admirable and even necessary to restrain karmic thoughts by will power, that alone will not really improve our life, purify our soul, or decrease our karma.

Clearly distinguish the real you from your karmic thoughts

This is why I always urge people to clearly distinguish between their true self and their karmic thoughts. Any display of emotions, if they are hurtful to yourself or to others, should be controlled temporarily by will power. Even if you have been unable to hold these emotions in check and they have shown themselves on the outside, thrust them away without adhering to them, recognizing them as the reverberations of your karmic thoughts from past existences, appearing now in order to vanish away forever. It is good to do this as soon as the emotions calm down, though it is even better to do so while the emotions are still raging. As you cast the emotions away, direct your mind to thoughts of thankfulness toward your guardian divinity and guardian spirits. To do this requires constant training of your thoughts, but it will enable you to exit from the swirl of karmic thinking faster than with any other spiritual method, so that you can always keep your thoughts united with your true self (God).

One cannot become good at anything without practice and training. Therefore, do not be discouraged if you are defeated by your karmic thoughts two or three times. Just continue to thank your divine and spiritual protectors, and try not to attach yourself to the karmic thoughts that emerge. Rather, remind yourself that they are vanishing away.

However deeply rooted the emotions may be, and however dark the circumstances, they will absolutely vanish if you continue to practice this method. In this way, you can reunite with your true, divine self during your present physical lifetime.

God never torments human beings

Since God is the great parent of human beings, God wishes for our happiness even more than our physical parents do. Under no circumstances does God ever inflict punishment on weak, physically-oriented human beings, nor does God hurt or torment them.

It is a matter of course that we should have reverent feelings toward God, but there is no need at all to fear God or think that God is far away from us. It is the love of God that gave shape to our guardian divinities (or angels) so that they could closely protect and encourage us human beings. In this way, God is enabling physical human beings to construct a joyful world.

If you are leading an unhappy life, it is not because God is punishing you. It is because you have been living, from past times up to the present, in separation from God without knowing the truth.

Even if you go to churches, shrines, or temples, that in itself does not mean that you believe in God. A person who truly believes in and reveres God must, first of all, believe in God's love, and also believe himself or herself to be a spirit from God, born in this world for the fulfillment of some kind of mission.

Since we do not exist separately from God, but are surrounded, both within and without, by God's life, the wise way to live is simply to concentrate on thankfulness toward God and toward all things. This way of living is much closer to God than the practice of merely going to temples and shrines or attending religious services.

The mentality of a person who feels resentment and jealousy toward others, finding fault with them in every detail, yet all the while aspires to receive special favors from God, is a very foolish one indeed. These are karmic thoughts of a most grievous kind.

God is love, and human beings are brothers and sisters in life. (The reason why I say 'in life' is that people are not brothers and sisters in terms of their karmic thoughts or their karmic cause and effect.) Shall we not pray for the peace of the world, so that the mission of earthly humanity may be fulfilled as soon as possible?

SPIRITUAL AWAKENING

I am sometimes asked what it means to be spiritually awakened. 'Spiritual awakening' and 'enlightenment' are terms that no one seeking truth can be indifferent to.

Because people long for spiritual awakening, they seek a path to truth and search for teachers to guide them. Their desire for spiritual awakening is what motivates them to join religions, spiritual groups, or organizations pursuing moral cultivation, and to undergo various kinds of discipline and training. However, we occasionally come across people whose actions come from an awakened spirit, yet it never occurs to them that they are awakened—nor do they even desire or try to be!

In Japanese, the character for 'awakening' is 悟 (pronounced *satori*). It is composed of two parts: (心), meaning 'heart' or 'mind,' and (吾), meaning 'I' or 'self'. When the two are combined into one character, it means 'unity of self and mind.'

Most people think of their minds as a separate, distinct part of themselves. They say 'my mind' as if it existed somewhere inside the 'self,' which is quite illogical. Without the mind, how would anyone be able to recognize the self's existence? Since the mind exists first, and has the capacity to recognize the self, we would do better to say that the self is something located at the periphery of the mind—an outer shell around the mind.

Practically speaking, then, the mind must actually be the self. Yet if so, why does it frequently happen that even though the mind says not to, a person does bad things, such as drinking too much, getting angry, or bearing grudges against others? One part of the mind is warning against it, and another part is doing what it should not do. This is quite a mysterious phenomenon. Which of these two mentalities is the true one? Which of them is the true self, the real you?

The origin of the mind

Before we can answer this question, there is something else that we must think about: did the mind come into existence when the physical body was formed, or did it exist beforehand?

If we say that the mind came into being at the same time as the physical body, we have to recognize the existence of a creator-like being with superior wisdom who arranged for its conception, its growth in the womb, and its birth into this world. Certainly, a human being, possessing a wondrous intelligence like ours, could not have been produced by a mere substance or wave that has no intrinsic wisdom. Even if people pooled all their knowledge to build the best machine they could, that machine could never produce a human being. After all, a machine is never more than a created object. Likewise, there is no doubt that the physical body housing a human being is also a created object, made by a being with great wisdom who existed beforehand.

When human beings construct machines, they wish to freely use them for their own purposes. In the same way, it is certain that the existence who created physical human beings also intended to activate them with a particular objective in mind.

In view of this, what would happen if we physical human beings kept on pursuing the freedom and happiness of our physical consciousness alone? Sooner or later, we might find ourselves unable to distinguish whether or not we were drifting away from the objective of our creator. In that case, there would be no assurance that humanity might not head off in a direction that was completely counter to the purpose we were created for by the being with great and absolute wisdom (God).

Now we have come to the point where spiritual awakening becomes an issue of great importance. It is also time to answer our question about the two mentalities of a human being. One of these is the divine mentality that is joined with the mind of the creator—God. This is the true mentality of a human being. It is an extension of the original divine life,[5] working here so that God's intention can be fulfilled in the world of human beings. Its existence can be traced back to a time before the birth of the physical body. The other mentality is the surface consciousness, composed of thought waves. In Buddhism it would be called *shiki* (識) or karma (業).

The true self, or true mind, is endeavoring to freely and smoothly activate the life that occupies the physical body, so as to carry out the work assigned to it under the universal design. However, after the formation of the physical body, human beings created a physical (material) consciousness, generating thoughts and feelings directed at enhancing their physical comfort and wealth rather than promoting the advancement of humanity. The karmic vibrations of this physical consciousness came to completely surround the true consciousness (true self). It assumed a personality of its own, and marched through human society declaring itself to be the true identity of a human being. From that point on, society took shape according to principles of materialism.

Thoughts and actions based on materialistic principles had the effect of driving humanity further and further from their divine nature, and they forgot about the mentality that existed before the birth of their physical existence. This led to the mistaken belief that the 'mind' first came into being along with the physical body.

This way of thinking, in itself, is the source of all human suffering. The disharmonious vibrations of humanity's thoughts and actions, based on its mistaken sense of identity, have produced a variety of conditions and events such as natural disasters, wars, social disorder, and struggles among individuals. These same disharmonious vibrations are what prevent each individual, and humanity as a whole, from building a truly happy life.

Now that we have come to the final days of material culture and civilization,[6] unless all human beings awaken to their true identity, humanity as a whole will meet with an enormous catastrophe that is heading toward us at this very moment.

From these explanations, I believe that you have gained a sense of the importance of spiritual awakening. Now let us explore the matter in a little more detail.

Anger and fear are not the true you

To be awakened is to be perfectly unified with your true self. It is important for you to clearly recognize and affirm that when you experience feelings like anger, resentment, jealousy, sorrow, fear, or attachment, they do not come from your true self.

It is also important to affirm that your true self is one and the same as God, and that the miscellaneous thoughts that travel through your surface consciousness are the aftermaths of things you mistakenly thought and did in the past. They are taking shape now for the purpose of vanishing into nothingness.

You need to know that you are your own creator. What this means is that you are one member of a divine group that came down from the heavenly world for a particular purpose; you are working here so that the divine life of the universe can bloom and flourish in the earthly world.

To be awakened is to let your true self shine—it is to fully activate your life without any hindrance. There are many stages of awakening. If you can give expression to your true self for just a brief moment, fully utilizing your life-energy for your divine purpose, this is one form of awakening. If you consistently exhibit your true, divine nature at all times, it can be said that you are a perfectly awakened one, like Buddha or Jesus Christ.

What kind of life is led by a person who always gives direct expression to his or her true self? Such a person has great depth of love, and is never ruled by turbulent emotions. He or she is without fear, and can always perceive the divinity in others, clearly distinguishing it from the flow of people's surface thoughts. An awakened person naturally and spontaneously purifies the thoughts of others without even thinking about it.

Another way of writing 'awakening' is with the character (覚), symbolizing the condition of being awake and of correctly perceiving the essence of one's mind. To correctly perceive the essence of one's mind is to be awakened in the correct sense of the word. This is the same thing as living from the perspective of your true self.

Your true self, or true mind, is God—the divine mind. Since God is light, when you live though your true self, your whole being shines. This light is visible to people with psychic perceptions, and it is felt by others through the atmosphere that you project. When you are awakened, or are coming close to that state, your inner light cannot help reflecting itself in your daily speech and behavior.

There is only one mind

Thus far, I have been talking about two minds, but in the ultimate sense there is only one mind—the true mind, the mind of God. The surface consciousness, which is often called the 'mind,' consists of nothing more than thought waves, which are impermanent by nature. In simple terms, a thought wave (vibration) generated in the past acts as a cause, which later touches against an inducement (trigger), and produces a certain effect. This process is known as cause and effect.

During the course of history, people mistakenly began to refer to the activity of their thought waves as their 'mind.' This misunderstanding produced a distortion in the proper functioning of life.

Life is something that comes from God. The true mind of a human being works so as to smoothly put life into action exactly as it comes to us from God. When the true mind of each individual activates the functions of life, our combined activities will cause a world of great harmony to appear immediately. However, at the present time, the activity of each person's thought waves (karma) is following its own willful course, and this inhibits the proper resonance of life.

In order to make a peaceful and happy world, it will be necessary for each individual to live their lives in a way that agrees with the mind of God. The mind of God is love, brilliant light, and harmony. This is the original mind of a human being. Consequently, we can say that any thoughts that depart from love, light, and harmony are thoughts that are removed from God. This makes them illusory thoughts.

Medical scientists say that thoughts and feelings like anger, struggle, fear, jealousy, and sadness pollute the blood and disturb its circulation. This means that they disturb the flow of a person's life. Furthermore, those thoughts and feelings also emit waves that are transmitted to the people around us, our society, and all humanity, exerting a negative effect on our world. Thus, one individual's thoughts influence not only that person, but others as well.

Hônen and Shinran

On the other hand, if even one person develops their spirituality, letting their thoughts be transformed by the brilliant light of their true mind, it will have the effect of purifying society and humanity as a whole, even though the person involved may be unaware of it.

Since ancient times, many people have lived in the mountains and undergone severe ascetic disciplines so as to become spiritually awakened, but very few of them have come close to that state. The priest Hônen,[7] founder of the Pure Land sect of Buddhism, was a person of profound learning beyond comparison with any of his contemporaries, and he also underwent every kind of *Shôdômon* discipline[8] practiced by the ascetics of his time. Even so, he was unable to feel wholly at peace, nor could he attain a feeling of true security. Through his anguish, Hônen realized that however profound his learning and however strict his ascetic practices, they would never enable him to reach spiritual awakening. As long as his consciousness and the state of awakening itself remained separate, he would never awaken. He then knew that he must give up his desire for awakening and entrust all his thoughts to Amida Buddha,[9] who symbolized his true, divine self. Thus he began to intently call upon Amida Buddha at all times, without even the briefest interval, so as to unite his consciousness with his true, divine self.

This was truly a great thing. It was indeed remarkable for a priest with such profound learning as Hônen's, who had gone through such extensive ascetic discipline, to discard his learning and all his training methods and completely believe in the existence of Amida Buddha, whom no one had ever seen, and in the Western Pure Land, to which no one had ever been.

This is by no means as easy as it seems. If a person were illiterate, poverty-stricken, or seriously ill, it might not be difficult to plunge into such wholehearted belief, but for someone in Hônen's position it was nothing short of an act of great courage.

In the *Dai-Muryôjukyô* (Infinite Life Sutra or Larger Sutra on Amida Buddha), there is a teaching called 'The vow of Hôzô Bodhisattva'[10] (the original vow of Amida), which goes like this: Hôzô Bodhisattva vowed that if he became fully awakened he would become Amida Buddha in the Western Pure Land, and would come to the rescue of anyone who called his name. However, since Sakyamuni Buddha was no longer alive at that time, and the Buddhist sutras were not written by Sakyamuni himself, there is no assurance that this teaching is true. One can confirm theoretical and philosophical scriptures, but since this scripture is just a story, there is no concrete evidence to be relied on. Therefore, one can simply choose whether to believe it or not. Why, then, did such a learned scholar as Hônen devote his life to this teaching after all his profound studies?

Now, as I envision the mind of Saint Hônen, I can understand well the feelings that he experienced at that time. Hônen himself was surely aware that, among the priests of those days, his learning was of a fairly high level (it was pre-eminent in the eyes of others). Yet he thought to himself: *If even I cannot awaken and live with a peaceful mind, how can the masses, who have less knowledge and social status than I, live in this world with tranquility and a sense of true spiritual stability? In my present state, I can do nothing for the deliverance of the general population. What am I to do?* Brooding over this question while reading a book, Hônen remembered the original vow of Amida that was written in the *Dai-Muryôju* Sutra.

He then intuitively felt that he had hit upon the answer. He made up his mind that the only way to rescue the masses was to teach them the original vow of Amida.

Hônen was able to reach this decision because it came at the end of a long, long search. He remembered the original vow of Amida after studying all the Buddhist scriptures again and again, leaving nothing more to be learned in Japan. Since this was the conclusion to his search, his thoughts had nowhere else to go after that, and so he concentrated perfectly on the original vow of Amida. From that time on, Hônen immersed himself body and soul in reciting the words: *Namu Amidabutsu.*[11] Put into modern language, this would be like thinking only: 'God and I are one' or 'I am in God.'

Previously, he had been seeking his awakening with his karmic thoughts, thinking that it could be achieved through learning, knowledge, or ascetic practices. But once he stopped chasing round and round in pursuit of it, and began to focus all his thoughts on Amida Buddha, to the extent that his thoughts merged with Amida Buddha, he was able to clearly discern his true self. Or, rather than saying 'discern,' it might be more accurate to say that he became more closely united with his true self.

In the case of Shinran,[12] he went one step further, fully discarding all thoughts and entrusting everything to God through the name of Amida Buddha, paying no attention at all to the activity of karmic thought waves. His method was one of total reliance on the divine. Since Hônen was the first to advocate the practice of reciting *Namu Amidabutsu*, he needed to make great efforts to do it. But his disciple Shinran, having his respected teacher, Hônen, close at hand, needed only to believe in the teaching and put it into practice. From the time when he first believed in it, he threw himself fully into the recitation, completely entrusting everything to God without even the slightest element of self-power (see chapter 6).

Before he met his teacher Hônen, Shinran had gone through all the same ascetic practices that Hônen had. That is why he, too, could plunge himself into the recitation of *Namu Amidabutsu* as Hônen had done. Shinran felt that since his thoughts (not his mind) were so erroneous and so filled with mistaken ideas, there was no hope at all of remedying them. He felt that he would never awaken spiritually until he separated those thoughts from himself, and so he gave up on his former 'self' as being thoroughly useless and sinful. He likewise gave up his conscious search for an awakening. In discarding everything about his former 'self,' he was able to throw his life wholly into the recitation of the *Nembutsu* from the day of his first encounter with Hônen.

After that, Shinran's faith included no element of struggle or strain, no quest for knowledge, and no thoughts urging him to attain enlightenment. For Shinran, there was nothing left to do but live while thinking of Amida Buddha and calling Amida Buddha's name. He never thought that his ascetic discipline would uplift him, or that he would uplift others through his own conscious effort. He thoroughly believed that if he guided people toward the way of Amida Buddha, Amida Buddha would uplift those people in response to their own recitations.

What lay at the root of Shinran's faith was most certainly the distinction that he made between his true mind and his karmic thought waves. He clearly recognized that all the conditions that occurred in his physical life were manifested through the great merciful love of Amida Buddha. He recognized that all the pleasures and misfortunes associated with his physical existence were the manifestations of karmic causes from his previous existences and were now being extinguished by Amida Buddha. I think that the same could be said about Hônen as well. Their state of mind would correspond to the Christian prayer words '*Thy will be done*,' which are a prayer of complete entrustment.

Hônen and Shinran knew well what emotions are

The days of Hônen and Shinran were not like today, when freedom and equality are widely called for. In those days, the common people found themselves wedged in between the various people in power, and they felt no economic stability or emotional security in their lives. Never knowing what the morrow might bring, they always lived in trepidation, gasping under the threat of a crisis. In the society of their day, no matter how hard and honestly they might work, their hearts could never find tranquility. Thus, it is not difficult for us to imagine what peace of mind they felt from the Pure Land sect's teaching of deliverance in the next world.

For the general population, having no schooling and little knowledge, there was hardly any opportunity to grasp the complex teachings of Buddhist philosophy. Difficult theories like that of the Tendai sect were understood only by the cleverest among the court nobility, bureaucrats, and warriors; and since these understandings were merely theoretical, it seems to me that they could hardly have guided anyone to a state of mental calm or spiritual awakening. Even among monks and priests, only the rare ones of remarkably high character could have reached a state of spiritual peace and stability through those teachings.

Even though people might be instructed to eliminate their selfish desires, there is no reason to think that they can readily do it. Even though they might be told not to be fearful, angry, or sorrowful, and to refrain from attaching themselves to anything, there is no reason to think that tendencies like these can be so easily corrected.

Hônen and Shinran never said a word to people about remedying those kinds of emotions. Rather, they said to them: *In terms of our physical emotions, we are no different from you. Just leave your emotions be. Simply call upon Amida Buddha with all your heart. If you are angry, recite the words while you are angry. If you are crying, recite the words while you are crying. Just by doing this, you will be delivered into the Pure Land.*

Their way of explaining things shows us that Hônen and Shinran clearly knew how to distinguish between physical emotions (karma) and the true mind (divine mind).

Your physical thoughts and emotions are not something that can be extinguished through your own efforts unless you are a person of surpassingly high character. Instead of trying to do this, Hônen and Shinran simply let go of their physically-oriented thoughts, letting them spin round on their own, and devoted themselves to wholeheartedly reciting the *Nembutsu*, so as to unite their true selves with Amida Buddha.

In practicing this method, you let your true self merge with the world of Amida Buddha without pursuing your karmic thoughts at all. As a result, those karmic thought waves, carried over from a past consciousness, naturally vanish away and the light of your true mind—which is the brilliance of Amida—illuminates your life, and you can start your journey to the next world in a state of spiritual peace and stability.

The thought of being uplifted by Amida Buddha after death and being reborn in the resplendent Pure Land naturally made people feel that their chances of being rescued by Amida Buddha would be greater if they tried to live righteous lives, even while suffering from poverty, rather than pursuing worldly wealth and fame by doing iniquitous things. At the same time, their faith also considerably diminished their feelings of self-reproach for their own karmic thoughts. This was the Pure Land sect's true teaching of the recitation of *Namu Amidabutsu*—to let your true mind spontaneously emerge in your daily life without consciously striving for it through your own individual power (self-power).

For people who truly shared the mentality of Hônen and Shinran and faithfully practiced the *Nembutsu*, there was no doubt that the light of their true mind would reveal itself in their lives. However, if even the slightest thought of self-power were introduced, it would drag them down to a hellish condition where they would examine the behavior of others and criticize it, while also blaming and judging themselves for their own conduct. This would shatter the precious teaching of complete entrustment that was the Pure Land faith, and would result in conflicts among its believers.

A method of complete entrustment

When self-power is brought in, one is inevitably tempted to blame and judge others. When you consciously try to awaken yourself, the effectiveness of Amida Buddha's grace is considerably weakened. As long as you attach yourself to your own thoughts, there is no way for you to plunge into Amida Buddha, who exists beyond the realm of your karmic self. The recitation only comes alive for you when you turn away from that self.

If your recitation is accompanied by thoughts like *I am a bad person* or *I am awakened*, it is not authentic. The true recitation does not contain any thought of self-abasement or self-aggrandizement, either. It is no more and no less than a recitation of complete entrustment to Amida Buddha.

This principle was perfectly clear to Hônen and Shinran, both of whom had previously followed the path of self-power at great risk to their lives. Among their followers, though, there seem to have been fairly many who did not grasp the principle very well. As a result, those followers thought that they would awaken themselves with a combination of self-power and complete entrustment, practiced together.

On the other hand, those who were able to pray the *Nembutsu* with an attitude of complete entrustment were surely able to convert their faith to actual practice, and they could proceed along their path to truth without losing their footing. This is because when our mind stays attuned to Buddha, the integral perfection of Buddha will inevitably flow straight into our mind. It is not because we will it so with our conscious thoughts. When our mental waves are joined with Buddha, a way of living that closely corresponds to the mind of Buddha naturally manifests itself in our life.

This is just like saying that when we look at the moon, only the moon comes into view. The moonlight is not overwhelmed by the light from the faraway stars, and when we look at the moon, we are not admiring the faraway stars. In the same way, when we focus our attention only on Amida Buddha, we are not be influenced by the dark clouds that are separate from Amida Buddha's light. Should bad conditions appear, like dark clouds in the sky, it simply means that karmic thoughts from our past are in the process of vanishing. It is certain that they are not being newly created just now.

The claim of Nichiren

However, after the deaths of Hônen and Shinran, many people in the Pure Land sect misunderstood the *Nembutsu* recitation. Some produced new karmic thoughts as they recited the words without sincerity. Others, who could not clearly see the distinction between their true self and their karmic thoughts, recited it for the sake of their karmic desires for wealth and fame. Wholehearted devotion to the *Nembutsu* became a rarity.

At that time, the priest Nichiren[13] came on the scene and declared that salvation through the *Nembutsu* was totally out of the question, and that the people who recited it would surely fall into the deepest layers of hell.

Nichiren's claim was that the only Buddha in this world was Sakyamuni Buddha, and that it was an untruth to say that there was a Buddha called Amida who would save people. His exclamations went like this: *What will*

save people and save this country is none other than the Lotus
Sutra, the final teaching of Sakyamuni Buddha. All the teachings
that came beforehand were, as Sakyamuni Buddha himself said,
preludes to that teaching, and were in themselves only the means
to an end. Consequently, all those who believe that salvation
can be attained through expedient measures will fall into hell.
If everyone held such beliefs, the nation would come to ruin. He
then added a warning that Japan was at that very moment
under threat of such a crisis.

Although there was some logic behind Nichiren's argu-
ment, the main drawback was that the deep truth within
the Lotus Sutra was at that time incomprehensible to the
general population. However, since Nichiren's mind was
filled with the desire to uplift Japan as a nation, his first
priority was to make the Lotus Sutra known to the chief
politicians and people in power rather than to the general
population.

Nichiren's outcry was for saving the nation first, rather
than oneself. This was how he came to boastfully refer to
himself as 'the pillar of Japan.'

The essence of 'Buddha'

Since Hônen and Shinran aimed at the deliverance of individuals and Nichiren aimed at the salvation of the nation,
it was inevitable that their methods would differ.

As for Nichiren's claim that the followers of Hônen's
teaching were all bound for hell, this was something
that Nichiren thought of all by himself and there was no
truth to it. It could never happen that such a great saint as

Sakyamuni Buddha could, even as an expedient, set forth a teaching that would drive people into hell.[14] Each human being comes into this world with their own propensities and talents, and each must be given a teaching that is appropriate for them.

To Hônen, who taught of Amida Buddha in the Western Pure Land, and of the deliverance to be reached by reciting his name, it was not really an issue whether there was a Buddha named Amida or not. I think he only utilized the original vow of Amida, something he luckily found in the *Dai-Muryôju* Sutra, as a focal point so that human beings could concentrate on the concept of a perfectly harmonious and purified place, and on a personification of Buddha (God) who fulfilled their hearts' desires. He did this because, through any ordinary means, it would have been extremely difficult to separate people from the karmic thought waves that travel in and out of the brain without leading people to attach themselves to those mistaken thoughts. And so he left those thought waves to circulate on their own, and directed people's attention toward the heavenly Pure Land, where the perfectly harmonious Amida resides. The reason why he designated one particular place and limited the recitation to Amida Buddha was that if the people had only concentrated on their inner Buddha, or on Sakyamuni Buddha, they would not have been able to focus on one point, and their thoughts would have wandered. Once their thoughts wandered, they would be dragged down into the karmic whirlpools and would not be able to unite with Buddha.

A person of Hônen's calibre surely knew that 'Buddha'

is the perfect, all-encompassing power of life that exists in each individual and fills the universe. Yet having this knowledge rarely means that the power of life is freely manifested without the slightest hindrance. This is because the cycling movement of karmic thought waves that surround the true mind obstructs its perfect manifestation. To resolve this problem, Hônen focused all his consciousness on one point—the recitation of *Namu Amidabutsu*. Thus, he separated the cycling movement of his karmic thoughts from his true mind. In other words, his true mind was united with Amida Buddha and his consciousness was lifted to a dimension too high to be affected by those cycling thoughts. Consequently, his daily life was completely free from disturbance by karmic thoughts and he did not accumulate any more of them from then on.

After Hônen's mind was completely filled with the *Nembutsu* he became perfectly awakened. Explained in today's language, his mind was united with God, and it seems that he saw into people's minds as if looking in a mirror. With the absolute confidence that he gained through his own experience, Hônen led people to a world filled only with the thought of Buddha (the *Nembutsu*).

To put it in terms of Zen Buddhism, his mind was in the state of *Kuu*, or oneness with the true reality (Buddha). To attain this state of *Kuu* by Zen meditation, we must rise above many demonic realms without getting caught up in them. Since the ultimate goal is the state of *Kuu*, and we have to be constantly assessing, through self-power, in which direction it lies, we cannot become awakened unless we have a superior disposition and a very strong will. The Pure Land method, however, does not require the kind of will power that comes from self-power. Since the Pure Land method starts by recognizing the perfect and harmonious Pure Land of Amida, and focuses on it by means of uninterrupted recitation, it can be followed even by people who are not especially high in character, and it can more easily guide them to their spiritual awakening.

Since the Easy Path of the Pure Land was a method of complete entrustment to Amida Buddha, its believers could smoothly and tranquilly go along the road to their awakening without being in an elevated frame of mind. Nichiren, on the other hand, taught that all human beings are originally Buddha and are free from confusion, grief, and fear, and that such conditions are merely delusions. He explained that we are originally free Buddhas who can be neither burnt by fire nor drowned by water. Thus, his followers recite the words *Namu Myô Hôrengekyô*, declaring that they are from the perfect world of true reality, Buddhas from the very beginning, and their recitation has an exalted, spirited vibration.

This method does not teach reliance on any external power for being saved, or for entry to the path of spiritual awakening. There is no notion of progressing upward, either. It teaches that human beings are Buddhas from the very start.

Progress along the path that is just right for you

When we reflect on these various approaches, we realize that no true teaching can drive us into hell as long as we practice it correctly. However, if we practice it wrongly, we can indeed fall into a hell of some sort.

Since seekers after truth are entirely free to choose their own path, they should take the one that is just right for them. As for me, since I did not think that I was outstanding in nature, I chose the Pure Land method of complete entrustment, which also corresponds to the Christian approach, and it has brought me to where I am today. In this, too, I feel that I was wholly guided by my spiritual and divine guardians. In the future as well, I believe that these guiding spirits and divinities, who surround my divine self, will in some way work through my physical body for the benefit of other people and of the world.

To put it in terms of the Lotus Sutra, I, who am Buddha (my divine self or true mind) am letting the protective spirits and divinities in charge of guiding humanity work for the purification of humanity's illusory thoughts, or karma. Since both explanations describe the very same circumstances, I would suggest that you select the approach that best suits your way of thinking and put it into practice.

To sum up my thoughts, I do not feel that it is necessary for people to seek their awakening with their conscious self. All you need do is to clearly distinguish karmic thoughts from your true mind and live with gratitude to your spiritual and divine protectors, believing that all karmic, emotional thoughts and actions are destined to vanish away, and that the brilliant, light-filled world of your true self will naturally appear someday.

THE BRIGHT LIGHT
BEYOND THE SUBCONSCIOUS

What is the subconscious?

Although the term 'subconscious' is frequently heard these days, it is seldom used with an understanding of its true meaning. People tend to use the word quite casually, as if it had no particularly deep significance.

In the field of psychology, the functioning of the subconscious is considered to be extremely important. And as a person concerned with spiritual guidance, I also give serious thought to the activity of the subconscious.

Psychologists generally think of the subconscious as something that is formed only after we have been born in this physical world. They see it as containing our own thoughts and experiences, plus various influences received from our parents and the other people around us. Such is the prevailing view among psychologists today.

However, those of us who are concerned with spiritual questions think of the subconscious as something that existed prior to our physical birth in this present world. We interpret the subconscious as being the accumulation of our thoughts and actions carried over from many past existences. It includes not only thoughts and actions from our present lifetime, but also from our previous lifetime, and the one before that, and the one before that, and so on.

The human consciousness and human thoughts are composed of many complex elements. They include the apparent thoughts that we are presently aware of, and they also include the subconscious strata, where our past thoughts and deeds are concealed. In addition, they also reflect the spiritual consciousness (which includes the activity of our guardian spirits and guardian divinities). On top of these, there is also the divine consciousness—the resonance of our original mind.

People who are indifferent to spiritual questions think of the human mind in a simplistic way, and they never imagine it as holding such complex functions. This single misconception gives rise to the various kinds of tragedies that occur in human life.

On the other hand, there are also people who are extremely interested in spiritual questions, but have little knowledge as to the workings of the human consciousness. Due to their insufficient understanding, these people tend to rush head on toward a particular spiritual objective that they have idealized. In fixing upon their ideal, they try to suppress their own thoughts and actions, as well as the thoughts and actions of others. In this way, they try to chain themselves and others to what they regard as the ideal spiritual condition to be aimed for. Although they appear to be good people, what they are doing is, in reality, quite feckless. They are like mountain climbers who only possess knowledge of the summit of a mountain, without knowing how to climb it or what route to follow. They merely set their sights on the summit and rashly head toward it. This results in excessive labor for them, and they get overly tired and drop out along the way, or else they have to return to the foot of the mountain and start the climb all over again.

We do not think with our surface mind alone

What, then, is the function of the subconscious?

A human being's thoughts are mysterious indeed. The thought that has just come up in your mind is hidden somewhere the next moment, and then the next thought appears. The greater part of yesterday's thoughts are hidden in the shadows of today's thoughts. While a portion of our consciousness and thoughts from the previous year, or the year before that, might, by some chance, unexpectedly rise to the surface from time to time, most of them remain hidden somewhere.

How can we explain the functioning of the conscious mind? For what reason does it consciously recognize something at this moment in time? Let us suppose that there is an object, such as an apple. If we have never before seen or heard about an apple, we cannot recognize the object as an apple. The fact that we recognize it as an apple is doubtlessly because we have seen an apple at least once before, or else we have heard about its color and shape from someone. This means that the color and shape of an apple, recorded in our mind in the past, rise to the surface of our mind the instant we see one, causing us to recognize it as an apple.

Looking at it this way, we can conclude that when we recognize something or think of something, our past consciousness and past thoughts, which are usually called the subconscious, have been drawn out by some object or condition, and have floated up to the surface. They become a part of our conscious mind again, so that we recognize the object or the condition which has triggered them. What this means is that we cannot recognize a thing or think a thought with the conscious mind alone. The conscious mind cannot function independently of the subconscious mind.

Let us take the example of a woman who is now thirty years old. This person's experiences, formed by her thoughts and actions during the thirty years since she was born in this world, are hidden behind her surface consciousness and surface thoughts. They are each waiting for their turn to come out and reappear in the conscious mind. To explain it more deeply, the woman's experiences from the past thirty years, plus additional experiences from her previous existences, are piled up and hidden beneath the conscious level.

The mind which makes itself known on the surface is extremely slight, while the hidden mind is billions or trillions of times greater. Even this is an understatement. So great is its accumulation that we cannot really grasp how much has been accumulated and hidden there.

The subconscious determines the course of a person's future life

This is why the subconscious, or hidden mind, becomes an issue of great importance for human beings. To put it more emphatically, I would even say that the thoughts which are recorded there are so important that they actually determine the course of our future life.

No matter how hard we might think and exert ourselves at present, trying to improve our mind and make a better life for ourselves, we will run into difficulties if our subconscious harbors the sort of dark and rebellious thoughts which lead us toward discontent. To put it more precisely, if our subconscious holds thoughts of material attachment, thoughts affirming misery, and thoughts of anger, jealousy, sorrow, and laziness, misfortunes and defects will take shape in our future life in proportion to the degree to which those kinds of thoughts have accumulated in our subconscious. This can make it quite difficult for us to correct our faults and catch hold of good fortune.

The subconscious cycles naturally from the interior to the surface, like the wheel of a powered motor. After one of its recordings appears in the surface mind—in our consciousness or in our actions—that thought or action returns to the interior, forming a new subconscious recording.

Thus, even though we might presently feel that it is

not good to become angry, we might still become angry when incited by another person or group. This does not mean that we have created our anger now. Rather, angry thought waves have been drawn out of our subconscious by thought waves existing in the other party. Those angry thought waves then erupt in the form of our present anger.

A person whose subconscious holds no thoughts of anger, or else very few of them, has few or no thoughts of anger to be brought out by another party's anger-inducing waves. Consequently, anger will not occur in that person's surface thoughts and actions.

It is true that a human being can at times be free (or nearly free) from all thoughts. But if we do attain this state of void or near-void, we remain in it for only the shortest fraction of a second. Our 'empty' state of mind is then broken by the objects in the external world, or else by the inner movement of our own thoughts, leading us to see, hear, feel, or think something. The thing which we have thought or felt enters our subconscious, just as it is, forming a thought or action in our future. This is how the course of our future life is formed.

The way we live in our later years is the sum of our thoughts and actions from our middle age, youth, child-hood, infancy, and pre-infancy (previous existences).

For example, an elderly man who is now dying in the midst of misfortune is leaving this world while exhibiting the results of his past thoughts and actions, including those carried over from previous existences. Whether or not the man dies knowing this truth will make an enormous dif-ference as to his progress in the subconscious world.

Recognizing and rising above past mistakes

If, even at the last moment, this elderly man wakes up to reality, it will spare him much trouble and unhappiness when he goes to the next world. In saying 'reality,' I am referring to the reality of human existence. A human being is not simply a physical body, but is the very life of the universe (God), born into this physical world in order to carry out one role in the overall plan of the universe. After accomplishing this role, or mission, each of us then takes on a new mission in the next world, learning and experiencing a variety of things. Eventually, by means of these various missions and experiences, we finally arrive in a world where all the inhabitants have fully developed their divine consciousness—the consciousness of God.

If the elderly man recognizes this truth, and breathes his last breath with thoughts of thankfulness, thinking:

Ah... the accumulated recordings of thoughts and actions from my past lifetimes are being dispelled along with the demise of my physical body. Soon I will arrive in a new world, and will be given a new mission to carry out under the guidance of my guardian spirits and divinities (angels). How happy I am!

his subconscious will be purified, and he will be elevated by all the pains and hardships he has experienced so far. In another world, or else in his next lifetime, he will be able to place himself in a situation where he can give expression to the brilliance and splendor of God, the origin of the universe.

In general, though, it seems that most of the elderly people who have considered themselves to be unhappy just greet their death with sad thoughts, grieving over their misfortunes in this world. Because of this, when they go to the next world they again have to place themselves in a lifestyle which is far removed from their true identity.

Since our subconscious recordings are not contained in the functions of the physical body, but in the functions of the subconscious body, the fact that we have left our physical body does not mean that we have left our subconscious recordings behind. When we go to the subconscious world after death, the course of our life there will be determined by the thoughts and actions that were previously recorded in our subconscious body. If we remain unaware of the truth, it becomes necessary for us to be born once again in physical form, and to discipline ourselves by going through a variety of harsh and laborious experiences.

These harsh and laborious experiences arise through the natural rotation of thoughts and actions recorded in our subconscious. And, since they are products of our own creation, we have no grounds for reproaching God or blaming other people. If we blame and accuse others, those reproachful thoughts will come bouncing back to us in our future. This is the law of cause and effect. It means that if we do good things, good things will come back, and if we do bad things, we will reap the fruits of those harmful actions.

What, then, will happen to a person who has suddenly awakened to truth after doing all sorts of horrendous things, right up until the previous day? Even though, as of today, that person has started to act in the spirit of love, truth, and goodness, it might seem doubtful that he or she could ever find relief in this lifetime, owing to the heavy accumulation of negative thoughts and actions recorded in the subconscious. But such is not the case.

If we experience a feeling of repentance for our past actions and turn over a new leaf, our deliverance will be assured at that very moment. This is because, from this moment forward, we will accumulate no more negative recordings in our subconscious. If we can patiently endure our circumstances for a while, we will be able to forge a bright and peaceful environment—a world composed of good and good alone.

Avoid the track where the subconscious circulates

Here, I would like to touch briefly upon the kind of people whom I mentioned earlier as being highly interested in spiritual questions, but as having little awareness of the functioning of the human consciousness. As I noted above, these people are generally considered to be good people. However, in their enthusiasm to place themselves and others in an ideal spiritual condition as quickly as possible, they try to suppress everything that runs counter to their ideals. Because they do not know the truth of spiritual faith, the truth of human life, or the functioning of the subconscious, these people are committing an enormous blunder.

If a negative thought, such as anger, jealousy, fear, or

misery has now floated into the physical brain, this does not mean that the thought has just been manufactured in the physical body at this moment. Rather, this thought is something that has been naturally propelled outward from the subconscious, as if by a powered rotor. It moves with such force that however you might try to stop it, it will not be held back. The more you try to stop it or hold it down, the stronger its resistance becomes. Therefore, if you try to forcibly repress the thought, and even if it seems that you have been successful in doing so for a while, the thought has merely been compressed. Sooner or later, triggered by some occasion or circumstance, the thought will surely rise again to the conscious level, erupting with redoubled intensity.

This is just as if you were standing in the midst of traffic, with a continuous line of motor-powered vehicles moving in your direction. Even if you were able to hold back one or two of the vehicles, how could you stop all the others which continued to move rapidly toward you? It is certain that, in the end, you would be sent flying by a group of them rushing toward you with tremendous force. If you were to do such an ill-advised thing, what should have ended in a minor injury would turn into a major one.

If you found yourself in this situation, the ideal solution would be to avoid the route of the vehicles. Or, if this could not be done, the next best alternative would be to get out of the way each time a vehicle came toward you.

In terms of a human being's thinking, what are we to do when unharmonious thoughts or circumstances, recorded in the subconscious, rise to the surface? As in the above example, the thing to do is to avoid the route where those subconscious recordings circulate. How can we do this? It is here that spiritual faith begins.

The method of complete entrustment

The unharmonious thoughts and actions that were gener-ated by a person's material consciousness are continually circulating within the confines of three worlds. These three worlds are the physical world, the subconscious world, and the outer edges of the spiritual world. The worlds existing beyond these three are outside the circu-lating route of those recorded thoughts and actions.

What I recommend is for people to practice exercises that will enable them to exit from that route as quickly as possible. How can we free ourselves from those circu-lating thought waves? As my long-time readers are well aware by now, the method I recommend is for people to borrow the power of their guardian spirits and divinities (angels), who are beyond the reach of those circulating waves.

Each and every human being is watched over and pro-tected by his or her own guardian spirits. Our guardian spirits are our spiritual forefathers and foremothers, who have taken on the job of watching over and guiding their descendants. We could think of them as 'spiritual grand-parents.' These spirits, after their death in the physical world, were reborn into various realms of the spiritual world, where they underwent a variety of experiences.

Through these experiences, they attained a high degree of spiritual awakening, and are able to guide their descendants toward a happier future.

Over and above the guardian spirits, there is a guardian divinity who is working to protect that one human being. A guardian divinity could be described as a divine light radiating from the direct source of human life. In Japanese, the word for this direct source of human life is written in two characters. The first character (直, *choku*) means 'direct,' or 'directly emanating,' and the second character (靈, *rei*) means 'spirit' or 'spiritual energy.' This is the origin of our own life, and it is also the origin of the activities through which the vast, all-encompassing life works upon the human world.

Each person's guardian divinity and guardian spirits are continually working to purify the contents of that person's subconscious, allowing genuine intuition to come resonating through from his or her true mind (God). This is how they guide the person toward a better future. For this reason, it is of first importance to practice directing our thoughts to our guardian spirits and guardian divinity.

It is only natural for a person's spiritual grandparents to be concerned about their own grandchildren, and to pray for the betterment of their future. They always continue to protect you, whatever you might be thinking. However, if you constantly give thanks to them, your thoughts will firmly unite with theirs, and it will become much easier for them to protect you. At the same time, their work will also become more satisfying for them.

To give you a general overview, the human worlds could be broadly classified into three divisions. First, there is the 'divine world.' This is the realm of the spirit emanating directly from God, and it also includes our guardian divinities. Next, there are the spiritual and the subconscious worlds. The guardian spirits travel back and forth among the spiritual and subconscious worlds, purifying the accumulated thoughts of human beings with their light waves. Thirdly, there is the physical world. Although the thoughts that human beings emit while living in the physical world have the capability to move about freely in the subconscious, spiritual, and divine worlds, people usually limit their thoughts to the physical, or material realm. In view of this, I am trying to make it easier for people to direct their thoughts to the spiritual and divine worlds. But if I simply tell people to think of God, many of them will find the thought of God somewhat vague and difficult to focus on.

In the true sense, human beings are no less than spirits emanating directly from God. Originally, we are as God is. When we are able to reach the state of *Kuu*, having eliminated all the desires of the ego, or material consciousness, we can do just as God does, even while retaining our physical bodies.

In actual life, however, there is virtually no one who can do this. For example, we might try to convince ourselves that we are the perfect image of God from the eternal past to the eternal future, just as is written in the Lotus Sutra. However, our thoughts of trying to convince ourselves create an obstacle in our consciousness. Because of this obstacle, the image of God does not reflect itself in our actual circumstances. Although the truth is that human beings are the perfect image of God from the eternal past to the eternal future, it occasionally happens that people overstrain themselves in trying to reveal the image of God. In such cases, they are likely to take on an eccentric and peculiar atmosphere.

Project the divine image just as it is

The image of God is God's own likeness, reflected just as it is. However, when there is any element of distortion in the reflection process, the image of God can no longer be perceived. The image being projected is no longer 'as God is.'

To be 'as God is' is not easily achieved. Thoughts of disappointment, thoughts of greed, thoughts of elation, and thoughts of sorrow are not 'as God is.' The origin of a human being is life itself. Its image is what I call the 'spirit emanating directly from God.' This is the image of God, just as God is.

To reflect the image of God is to free ourselves from all egocentric thoughts and all thoughts and emotions relating to the material world, whether sadness or gaiety, anger or amusement. It is to shed all preoccupation with our material circumstances, so that our thoughts always live in the divine world. This condition is beyond the reach of any theoretical discussion or any probing of the subconscious. Until we let our thoughts and actions spring from a point further upstream than the subconscious, coming from the ancient self, the true self—the true image of God—will not be perceived.

Good people must live with dignity and courage

Therefore, I do not tell people to empty their minds of all thoughts, or to eliminate their self-oriented ambitions all at once. Nor do I adopt the method of psychiatrists, psychoanalytically delving into a person's subconscious in search of the causes of the thoughts and emotions (anger, jealousy, and so on) that have appeared in the surface consciousness. I do not attempt to stir up past mistakes made by that person or by others, nor do I want people to blame themselves or others for those mistakes.

Since all those emerging thoughts are the disappearing images of causes generated in the past, I advise people not to continue fixing their attention on those thoughts or circumstances. Rather, I advise them to turn their attention to their true selves (God), so that the bright energy of God can gradually fill their subconscious. If they are able to do this, little by little, their subconscious will be purified, and a better future will open up for them.

The more conscientious people are, the more they are inclined to focus on their mistaken thoughts and actions, and to chase after them. They may have a tendency to think: *Why do such bad thoughts* (anger, jealousy, selfishness, and so on) *always keep occurring to me, even though I am trying so hard to find the right way? I am just no good!* Next, they end up falling into an attitude of self-abasement and self-hatred, and gradually lose courage. If they go on living in this way, unless they have an exceptionally strong will and remarkable courage, they could become so timid in their daily thoughts and actions that they become unable to live life vivaciously, as their true selves would have them do. Despite their good intentions, they could end up confining themselves in the shells of their small ideas, and become unable to develop into people who attempt great tasks. Instead, they would find themselves overwhelmed by the driving force of audacious people whose thoughts are not attuned to the voice of their conscience. Thus, even though conscientious people wish to do good things, they can end up living their physical lives huddled up in a corner, resigning themselves to a lowly life of obscurity. It is a great loss for humanity that many good people cannot live their lives in this world with dignity and courage, the way that their true selves are living in higher worlds. This is something that distresses me.

It is important to try not to remain attached to any past thoughts, whether good or evil. The more we cling to the good or the evil of the past, the less free our mind is. And the more our mental freedom is lost, the less able we are to accomplish fine things.

Throughout history, a variety of spiritual leaders and teachers of moral cultivation have appeared to the world. Why is it, then, that the majority of good people still cannot live their lives with peace of mind? The reason is that good people have been too preoccupied with good and evil. This excessive preoccupation has hampered their natural power to act resolutely and decisively—which is to say that spiritual faith and moral cultivation have not been fully utilized in the social sphere.

Thank your guardian divinities and spirits

I would like to repeat here that the true mind and true body of a human being is a spirit emanating directly from God. The physical human being who now appears here is a composite of two aspects. One aspect is the true substance of a human being (God); the other aspect, sometimes called 'karma,' is the accumulation of thoughts and actions carried over from past existences.

In the original sense, we human beings are divine spirits who can freely communicate with one another. We came here, as individual physical human beings, from worlds of higher dimensions ('heavenly worlds') in order to depict the image of God in the earthly world. However, in order to reside in the material world, we inevitably needed to take on a material form—the physical body.

Since the spirits who came to earth were enveloped in restrictive, physical embodiments, they were not able to move as freely or as rapidly as their original selves could do. For this reason, they were not able to quickly build the divine realm that their true selves wanted to build. As a result, gaps were produced between their original intention and their actual performance. These gaps were expressed in the form of distorted, or incomplete, light vibrations. We might also describe them as 'light mixed with shadow.' These gaps have accumulated in the physical body (the conscious state) and also in the subconscious body (the subconscious state). These gaps are meant to be rectified as one stage in the creative process—the process of moving from incompletion toward completion. We can see this process going on in the still incomplete human world of today.

In terms of material creation, this incompleteness has been rectified to some extent. However, when it comes to human thinking—the mental sphere—its progress has been retarded. Instead of moving ahead on its own, the mental sphere is being dragged along by the trends in the world's material development.

The individual spirits (called human beings) who settled in the physical world are inevitably obstructed by the accumulated recordings of their past thoughts and actions, which continue to circulate in the subconscious state. Because of this, they are unable to do the work that their true selves want to do. Therefore, in order to help them, their guardian spirits and divinities always stay behind each physical human being, cooperating with them in order to completely manifest a divine realm on the earthly plane.

However, since the general population is largely unaware of this truth, they are making no effort to ask for the help of their guardian spirits and divinities. Nor do they send them any thoughts of appreciation. Instead, they sometimes fall into a mistaken attitude of resignation, thinking, *Well, that's life!* Or, they routinely take a materialistic viewpoint and try to control the material world with the force of their egocentric desires. (Refer to my book *God and Man*.)

If this continues, not only will humanity be unable to escape from the unsightliness of the struggles which have repeated themselves throughout history, but the earth itself will be destroyed by weapons such as nuclear bombs.

Now is the time when the whole of humanity—each and every one of us—needs to send all our thoughts back to our origin—the source of our life, God—so that the divine intention can be realized on this planet. And each one of us needs to ask for the help and protection of our guardian spirits and divinities, while thanking them and praying for the peace of the world. As we continue to do this, it is important for us to also regard all emerging thoughts and actions as the expressions of human beings' past mistakes, returning to us from previous existences. Instead of grasping at them, the thing to do is to push them aside and immediately redirect our attention to our true selves (God).

To always place your thoughts not in the midst of evil and misery, but high up in the perspective of God, is the best way to uplift yourself and uplift humanity.

PRAYER FOR WORLD PEACE

Kindly note that this chapter was originally written for a Japanese readership and published in 1960. We hope that its essential message may be appreciated by readers all over the world today.

Will the Earth be destroyed?

In a recent issue of *Shûkan Tokyo (Tokyo Weekly)* there was a headline reading "You Only Have Ten Years Left to Live!" in big, bold letters. A fortune-teller and a psychic had predicted that in ten years' time, the Earth was likely to be destroyed by nuclear weapons. That prediction, some scientists say, is not an impossibility if we human beings continue down our current path. At the same time, there are other scientists who brush aside this kind of prediction, calling it nonsense.

In reality, as we stand in the midst of a nuclear arms race, I think that people of all nations are bound to become quite anxious about nuclear weapons.

As it stands, the corporeal human beings who lead the major powers of this earthly realm, relying only upon their dysfunctional intellects to guide them, can think of only two ways to protect themselves: oppress their enemies with force or subdue them with psychological pressure. Thus, no matter how much smaller nations may beg or insist that the testing of nuclear weapons be stopped, their plea will never be answered. For those who are capable of looking at matters with calm objectivity, it is clear just how much these experiments hurt the human mind and body, and how utterly useless they are in forging a truly peaceful future. However, in the minds of those who lead the world's major powers amidst a maelstrom of conflicts and struggles, this logic is incomprehensible. They are rigidly convinced that there can be no other way to maintain a state of peace.

If we continue to produce these nuclear weapons we will, without a doubt, become unable to withstand the temptation to use them. This is human psychology, and it is also our karma. Just one small spark would be enough to turn the prediction in the *Tokyo Weekly* article into a reality.

The United States feels that it cannot sit idly by while the Soviet Union steadily draws smaller nations into its camp and attempts to further expand the communist bloc through a mix of cajolery and intimidation. However, America's 'peace offensive' (as odd a phrase as that is) is inferior to that of the Soviet Union. Thus, seeing no other means at its disposal, it feels compelled to use forceful intimidation to suppress the Soviet Union's advancement. Along with this, the United States also goes on to tell its smaller allied nations that it will be able to control the Soviet Union with its military power, and that other nations need not worry as long as they are allied with the United States. This perceived need to control smaller nations spurs the United States to continue producing and threateningly testing nuclear weapons.

On the other side of the table, the Soviet Union has deftly turned the methods employed by the United States to its own advantage. Even as it continues to produce a steady stream of nuclear weapons, the Soviet Union advertises that the United States is the aggressive party and poses the greatest threat to world peace. In its own 'peace offensive,' the Soviet Union declares that it has no ambition but to promote peace, and that it wants to walk hand in hand with all nations toward this aim. Thus, against the backdrop of its own power, the Soviet Union carries on negotiations with smaller nations for conditions favorable to itself in an attempt to manipulate those nations as it wishes.

No matter which side the smaller nations might choose, they are placed in a condition that is far removed from true peace. The issues of whether the Soviet Union will give up its ambition for world domination, or of whether the United States will call for a ban on nuclear weapons, are not something that smaller nations can say anything about. No matter what advice a third nation might give them, I do not believe it is likely that either country will attempt to change its underlying mentality.

In the end, I can only conclude that the power of the physical human consciousness, in and of itself, cannot possibly save the human race or avert the destruction of Earth.

Here in Japan, there are some well-informed persons who are truly concerned with the fate of their country and all humanity, and are working busily day and night in an effort to safeguard the world's future. Their understanding of world affairs, and of Japan's position, intensifies their concern about the confusion in today's world.

However, even these people do not know how to prevent the world from going to ruin. Every single day, they receive information that makes them uneasy. The more they understand the true world situation, the more it pains their hearts. Yet there is no definitive action they can take. All they can do is to congregate with others who think as they do and, for the time being, try to focus the minds of all Japanese people on a single, common goal.

Among these people, some might be conservatives, some might be socialists or communists, and some might be moderates. There might also be people of spiritual faith or religion. While these people worry about their country and the fate of humankind to the point that they can hardly eat or sleep, there are others who live without a care, never thinking about the human race or even their own country. Then, there are still others who feel such distress in their personal lives that they cannot spare a thought for their country or their society, let alone the whole world. Meanwhile, the Earth continues to silently support all these people's lives.

Will the Earth be destroyed in the near future, as prophets have long predicted, and as the article in *Tokyo Weekly* suggests? What, then, will be the future for humankind? I would like to share my thoughts on this topic as guided by my spiritual perception.

Only all-encompassing love can rescue humanity

I do not believe there is a single person—regardless of nationality—who does not wish for peace. Why is it, then, that the world is constantly engulfed in the terror of war? It is because, no matter what country they may live in, all people tend to put the interests of themselves and of their own country before everything else.

Until one's own interests, the interests of one's country, and the interests of other countries and humanity as a whole are seen as one and the same, we can never hope to achieve world peace. For example, if the United States, without thinking of its own interests or gains, supplied goods to non-affluent nations with no strings attached, those nations would be appreciative, and as a result would no longer keep one eye turned toward the Soviet Union. Today, however, the United States gives aid only on the condition of certain trade rules that are beneficial to itself. This kind of aid does not come from an expansive and loving heart. Countries that receive this aid have their hands tied and their freedom constricted by these trade rules and as such, they cannot simply enjoy the aid they have received. Naturally, they begin to wonder if the Soviet Union might offer them better treatment.

One may condemn this behavior on the part of the United States, but I believe that if we were put in the same situation, Japan would also require similar conditions to be met, and thus we are not qualified to speak out against it. With the present mental level of human beings, there is no country that would deal with other nations in a magnanimous and impartial way.

The Earth will never be destroyed

In today's world, international relations are nothing more than a large-scale tug-of-war over gains and losses. Countries with the most wealth and military power maintain the most advantageous positions, while less affluent countries with no military might must live in a constant state of intimidation. Under these conditions, we human beings will never attain our ultimate ideal of heaven on earth. If things remain as they are, Japan and other countries will have to choose to submit either to the United States or the Soviet Union. Even if Japanese people speak reminiscently of how things used to be, the fact is that we are now a small country with little wealth and military power, and no amount of wishful thinking can put us at the center of the world. This is a constant thorn in the side of many patriotic Japanese people.

Thus, the leadership conferred by wealth and military power exerts an overwhelmingly oppressive force on smaller, weaker nations. As yet, the greatest power of all—the true power of love and sincerity—is not being demonstrated by the people of any nation. As a result, just as past prophets have indicated, the time for the final battle between the two most powerful nations appears to be looming near, and the Earth seems destined to perish in the flames of nuclear destruction. However, through my spiritual perception, I can say with assurance that the Earth will never be destroyed.

Each of us is responsible

There are, in this present-day world, some highly evolved beings who are earnestly living by principles of truth, and guiding others with a correct understanding of spiritual faith. These people could be described as angels and bodhisattvas, sent from God in order to avert the destruction of Earth and uplift the consciousness of humanity. Here, I am not speaking of any particular religion. I am referring to anyone whose spiritual outlook is aligned with universal truth, and who puts those truth-filled beliefs into real practice.

These people know that individuals and nations are not meant to passively get through life by relying on others, or asking others to set things right. First and foremost, each of us must be aware that we are the ones who uplift ourselves and rescue humanity from the impending disaster. When every single person grasps hold of the truth that we are each responsible for safeguarding this world, we will be on our way toward that goal.

Upon hearing such words, many people might have no idea what to do, saying, *If we do not even know how to take care of ourselves and our children, how can we possibly take responsibility for all of humanity?* The method that I propose is an extremely simple and effective one. It is so simple that some might wonder how it could possibly be effective.

What is this method that can uplift both oneself and all of humanity? It is the steadfast practice of prayer—prayer for world peace. If anyone should be disappointed to hear that my method is based in prayer, then I think I can safely say that that person is unaware of the potential power of the human mind and spirit.

While I acknowledge that prayer is a part of all religious traditions and practices, I question how many religious leaders there are who are teaching true prayer. If people are not conducting their lives based on real, genuine prayer, then those people and the country they live in will eventually cease to exist. Genuine prayer is the only key to safeguarding the future of humanity.

If people go to church every day and faithfully read the Bible, while at the same time dropping bombs and continuing to produce more of them, their religious practice cannot be considered a true one. Nor is the faith of those who tremble with fear while they pray an example of true faith. As I have stated before, prayer is a declaration of life. To pray is to become life itself. To become 'life itself' is, in other words, to become one with God. Is there any other way to embrace and protect the world than to become one with God? I positively assert that there is not.

Our lives originate in the divine mind

The reason why the world has been driven into its present crisis is that human beings have separated themselves from God, the divine mind. The further we distance ourselves from the divine mind, the harder it is for us to communicate with each other, and the less able we are to trust one another.

The basis for this reasoning is that God is life and mind itself. Human beings are one within the life and mind of God, which is great love itself. Thus, as long as people remain distant from God, they can never truly become one with each other. Any unity that we might achieve with a thought that is removed from great love will fall apart someday. This is because that kind of 'unity' stems from our mutual self-interest and greed. When those benefits are lost, or when our greed is unsatisfied, our sense of unity disappears. This applies both to individuals and to entire nations.

Any sense of oneness or cooperation that is founded on profit and greed is useless, no matter how many times it is repeated. As we waste time in this manner, the layers of karma—illusory thoughts that are separate from God (great life and great love)—grow thicker and thicker, distancing us further and further from God. Eventually, this turns into a battle between one mass of karma and another, leading to the ruin of the individual and of humanity.

As long as people remain unaware that all of us were born from the divine mind, how can humanity ever become unified in a state of great harmony? Only under the name of God (great life) can we truly become one. The people of today have forgotten this, and they are trying to bring humanity together by means of their confused, karmic thoughts, which inevitably lead them to the use of weaponry or deception. Such is the state of the truthless world we live in today.

In order to bring harmony and true oneness to humanity, each individual must bring his or her karmic thoughts back to God, achieving a spiritual rebirth as one divine life. The way to do this is by practicing true prayer. If we do not, this world can never be salvaged.

The reason why I am emphasizing prayer above all else is that I want to minimize the sacrifices that humankind will make, and the disasters that the world will suffer. Without true prayer, it is clear that humanity will have to experience the greatest tragedy it has ever known.

A prayer for world peace

Now, how does one go about performing 'true' prayer? What I propose is a prayer for world peace that goes as follows:

> *May peace prevail on Earth.*
> *May peace be in my home country.*
> *May our missions be accomplished.*
> *Thank you, guardian divinities and guardian spirits.*

These words of prayer connect us, as corporeal human beings, with the large spiritual and divine group that is working for the awakening of humanity. This group includes all the saints, guardian divinities, and our enlightened spiritual ancestors. Prayer for world peace links us directly with this immense cooperative body of light through an agreement made with the spiritual and divine worlds.

I have clearly confirmed this through my spiritual perception, and this great spiritual group is always working behind me. There are also many other people around the world with acute spiritual perception who are working together with this great body of light.

The time has come for human beings to exhibit our divinity while we exist on earth with a corporeal form. It is now time for us to become perfectly at one with our spiritual and divine selves, and to bring true peace to this world.

Difficult religious theories and religious groups that exist only for worldly gains are already losing their purpose in this time of crisis. If spiritual teachings do not guide people from worldly gains to a spiritual awakening, and from an individual awakening to the awakening of all humanity, then such teachings are useless in today's world.

I exist here to provide assistance to this confused world. The sentences I write and the words I speak do not come from a physical individual called Masahisa Goi. Rather, I elucidate truth as a vessel of the divine will.

The divine mind acts upon human beings

At all times, in all sorts of ways, without a moment's rest, the divine mind is acting upon human beings in order to awaken and uplift humanity. Working through various people and various circumstances, the divine mind is using all possible means to further this aim. Dividing itself into two functions—God as the great life and God as guardian divinity—the divine mind is working to manifest its true image in the physical world.

The misfortunes that fall upon human beings are by no means created by God. Our misfortunes and hardships are what take place when a teetering pile of human karma, or distorted thoughts, crumbles to the ground.

Wars, natural disasters, and all other negative phenomena are manifestations of humanity's karma, appearing in order to vanish forever. If we ever wish to escape from the fear of such phenomena, we must refrain from making contact with the spinning movement of this karmic activity.

How do we do this? The method I advocate is to intently and continually devote ourselves to a prayer for world peace, such as the prayer that I have proposed above. For a little while, I advise that you set aside your smaller-scale wishes for the comfort of your own household or the success of your business and simply pray for peace. As Koutaro Takamura writes in one of his poems, "I was born at a good time." This line perfectly describes the age that is upon us.

I was born at a good time. Yes, now is the time when you as a human being can perform the greatest possible task. The time has come when every single individual can do something for the benefit of humankind. The time has come when you can give full expression to your true nature.

You might be under the impression that you exist in this world only as a physical human being. But the reality is that the true you is also living in the divine world as a *chokurei*, or direct spirit. In a world without a speck or shadow of misfortune, you are living just as surely as you are living in this earthly world. The key to realizing this is also found in prayer for world peace.

Uplifting yourself and humanity at the same time

At all times, place all your thoughts within a prayer for world peace and give thanks to your guardian divinities and guardian spirits. While you sleep, while you are awake, at all times, practice thinking in this way. In doing so, you will be able to transcend the karmic realms that are filled with misfortune and malice, and before you realize it, your love and sincerity will grow deeper. At the same time, you will be sending out waves of light that will bring peace to all humanity.

If you feel doubtful of this method, just try it and see. Many of the people who have put my words into practice have achieved fairly high states of awakening. As you engage in regular prayer for world peace, you may notice that:

* You feel less caught up in the hardships and negative phenomena that appear before you.
* You feel less angry, envious, and impatient.
* You are more aware of the value of your own existence.
* You feel confident that things will not get worse but will only get better in your life.
* You are able to clearly distinguish your genuine, essential self from your karmic self.

This last benefit—clearly distinguishing between your essential self and your karmic self—is the greatest effect this prayer method will have on you as an individual. Your real, true self is always your life itself—it is always present within you. It never falters. Your karmic self, on the other hand, is an ever-changing, ephemeral being that appears and disappears. As you come to understand this more clearly, your mental state will naturally become pure enough to overcome any kind of suffering. Before you know it, you will realize that whatever hardship or suffering you might face, once it has appeared, it will invariably disappear. And all the while, your essential, divine self continues to shine eternally.

Furthermore, through your prayers for world peace, the illusory thoughts of all humanity are carried closer to the light of the guardian divinities and spirits, which enables those thoughts to quickly disappear. Then, by way of those purified thought waves, vibrations of spiritual and divine light will cleanse the earthly world. Large quantities of light will flow from heaven into the physical world, extinguishing humanity's karmic thought waves before they can lead to natural disasters or wars. In other words, divine love will be able to spread out across the physical world.

Prayer for world peace wields this kind of immense power—it is a method that can uplift both the individual and all humanity at the same time.

Try it for yourself. The effects of this prayer method will soon exhibit themselves in the physical world. To make this a reality even one day sooner, I urgently hope that each and every one of you will practice prayer for world peace.

SELF-POWER AND
OTHER-POWER

Two paths that lead to God

When people embark on a spiritual path, they first need to make a choice whether to rely on the power within their individual self or on a power external to the self. In this discussion, I will refer to the former (*jiriki* in Japanese) as 'self-power' and the latter (*tariki* in Japanese) as 'other-power.'

Nowadays, many people seem to be unclear about the difference between self-power and other-power. In fact, it is not unusual to hear certain people who belong to new religions nonchalantly claim that the religion they practice is a religion based on 'absolute power.' However, 'absolute power' is something that only those who have reached the most profound depths of spirituality can begin to understand and express, either through self-power or other-power. The words 'absolute power' can never be used in a casual manner. This is because absolute power is a capability and an activity that originates directly from the universal divine source. Therefore, those who are truly able to say that the teaching they practice is one based on 'absolute power' are those who have attained perfect oneness with the divine.

In every spiritual path, the ultimate goal is to manifest absolute, divine power in our words and actions. To reach this spiritual state, people choose to follow either a self-power approach or an other-power approach. In Buddhism, for example, the sect most representative of a self-power approach is Zen Buddhism. On the other hand, it could be said that Pure Land Buddhism is representative of an other-power approach. Likewise, Christianity is also an other-power approach. These two approaches are two different routes to the common goal of unity of the self and the divine, or the development of one's true mind. Though the paths people follow may be different, at the deepest level of spirituality they lead to the same answers. Nevertheless, we cannot say that it does not matter which approach a person chooses for spiritual development. This is because, depending on the person's disposition and propensities, it is often the case that the pursuit of one chosen approach will be ineffectual.

There is no doubt that people who follow a self-power approach and succeed in reaching the highest level of the teachings are truly outstanding people in a spiritual sense. When we read their words and learn of their deeds and the details of their arduous training, we cannot help but feel a deep sense of admiration. However, if we were told that we would not be able to develop our own spirituality or find oneness with the divine spirit unless we too endured the very same disciplines, the majority of people would probably hold back, believing that emulating these eminent individuals was beyond their abilities.

The austere path of self-power

We know of the high priest Hakuin, who is said to be largely responsible for the revival of the Rinzai Zen Buddhist sect. Traveling from mountain to mountain and valley to valley in search of a teacher to guide him in his spiritual growth, he persevered with his own very intense training and self-discipline. During this time, however, he came down with a debilitating case of tuberculosis, and his health eventually deteriorated to the point where no doctor, no matter how skilled, felt able to treat him. However, Hakuin could not let himself die in an incomplete state of spiritual development. With sheer determination, he rose from his sick bed and set out in search of a teacher who might be able to heal both the restlessness of his mind and the illness of his sick body. By this time, his illness was in quite an advanced state—what in today's terms would be described as a tertiary or near-death stage—but he set out once more, traversing steep mountains and deep valleys on a desperate pilgrimage to seek truth. To his dismay, none of the teachers he encountered had the knowledge or means to bring his body back to health or put his mind at ease. When he reached the mountains of Shirakawa,

Hakuin at last came across a hermit called Hakuyu Shinjin who taught him a method of deep meditation. Hakuin took up this practice of looking deep within oneself, and after three years was able to rid himself of his debilitating illness, which had been deemed incurable. To traverse the steep, rugged mountains of Shirakawa, Hakuin is said to have laboriously grasped tree roots and vines, and to have plodded long distances through deep snow and ice, which, needless to say, demanded extraordinary willpower.

After successfully attaining enlightenment at this risk of his life through this excruciatingly austere form of training, Hakuin went on to train disciples, exacting of them the same rigorous standards, and the Zen illness (tuberculosis of the lungs) is said to have been rife among his disciples. When one considers the relentless, austere training his disciples had to endure in conditions of both extreme heat and extreme cold, with little sleep or food, it is little wonder that one disciple after another fell ill.

One promising young prodigy among Hakuin's disciples, whose name was Suio, is said to have been caught in a struggle to resolve a *kôan*, or Zen parable. Despite his prolonged efforts, he had difficulty resolving it completely. When Hakuin saw Suio having such difficulty, he shouted at him, "If you cannot complete this task within seven days, you may as well throw yourself into the ocean and end your life!" When after seven days Suio still had not resolved the *kôan*, he did indeed throw himself into the angry waves of the winter sea, determined to die as he had been ordered. According to the story, at that very moment he succeeded in reaching great enlightenment and was later allowed to be in the company of Hakuin once again.

Thus, in the Rinzai Zen Buddhist sect individuals have the sheer determination to willingly throw away their lives and to wear themselves to the bone in relentless training that incorporates each and every action of their daily lives. Otherwise, not only will they fail to attain enlightenment, but they run a high risk of becoming hypocrites less worthy than ordinary lay people.

Dôgen Zenji, the founder of the Sôtô Zen sect, was also known to be severe and uncompromising with his disciples. On one occasion, Dôgen's disciple Genmei was asked by Hojo Tokiyori, who had deep admiration for Dôgen's moral excellence, to carry a letter to him in which Tokiyori expressed his desire to make a donation of land to Eiheiji Temple, where Dôgen resided. Genmei was elated that an official of such high rank as Tokiyori should show such admiration for his teacher, and felt very fortunate to be training as his disciple. He proudly took the letter to his teacher. Dôgen, however, far from being happy with the contents of the letter, cast the letter into the fire. He thoroughly rebuked Genmei for having such a low state of mind as to take pleasure in being offered material things, and told him that it could not be tolerated. He imposed the ultimate punishment on the disciple by dispelling him from Eiheiji Temple. It is also said that Dôgen did not stop there. He ordered the very spot on the floor of the meditation hall where Genmei had previously sat to be cut out and to have the soil underneath the hole dug out to a depth of three meters and carted away.

Dôgen's response may have reflected the depth of his spiritual purity, but his extraordinarily stern attitude is beyond imitation.

Is enlightenment through Zen meditation possible?

The teachings of Zen are so strict that unless the teachers of Zen adopt an attitude as uncompromising as Dôgen's, it is unlikely that any of them will attain enlightenment. This is because the manifestation of each person's inner Buddha, which is the essence of Zen Buddhism, is made possible only by the person's own power, without any reliance on others. On this point, Hakuin was very strict, and he severely denounced the practices of Nembutsu Zen, insisting that Zen Buddhism was not a combination of meditation and the chanting of holy invocations. From his viewpoint, the essence of Zen Buddhism was, purely and simply, to draw forth one's true self from within.

In short, Zen Buddhism is based on truth that is not attained with words, and on the direct transmission of this truth to reach enlightenment. It rules out any dependence on words or places and emphasizes achieving enlightenment purely through the individual practice of seated meditation.[15] That said, achieving enlightenment through meditation is no easy task, and so eminent priests like Dôgen and Hakuin had to go through extreme hardships to reach enlightenment. When we look at it this way, it is only natural to wonder whether the average person nowadays could achieve enlightenment in this way, solely through seated meditation. In my view, it is quite doubtful.

Indeed, the great teacher Dôgen himself said that it served no purpose for someone to engage in meditation with the aim of attaining Buddhahood or achieving enlightenment, or even with the aim of doing away with illusions and gaining insight into one's true nature. He maintained that a person who is wholly absorbed in Zen meditation, free of all thoughts, is already a sitting Buddha, just as he or she is. Dôgen was indeed correct on this point, and he was a truly exceptional person. However, even the very idea of achieving a state of no thoughts is something that I do not think can be accomplished simply through seated meditation.

Generally speaking, the more we sit and meditate, the more thoughts come into our minds, and the more confused we become as we struggle with thoughts of not thinking. The reality is that most of us do not even perceive the state where we can be free of ideas and thoughts, much less draw near to it.

Other-power as a road to freedom

Unlike Zen Buddhism, which focuses on meditation as the sole means of drawing out one's inner Buddha (divinity), the Jôdo, or Pure Land, sect of Buddhism accepts the limitations of human beings from the outset, recognizing that human beings are unlikely to reach enlightenment through their own efforts, no matter how hard they try. Instead, it teaches people to seek enlightenment by placing their faith in Amida, the Buddha who resides in the Western Pure Land. According to Pure Land Buddhism, Amida Buddha alone has the power to uplift and awaken human beings, and people who fervently and wholeheartedly recite the prayer *Namu Amidabutsu* will be accepted into the Pure Land. It is said that Amida Buddha does not consider the misdeeds that people may have committed in the past, nor what kind of thoughts they may have harbored in their minds. If they give themselves over to reciting the prayer *Namu Amidabutsu*, Amida Buddha will rescue them without fail, no matter how darkly clouded their pasts might be. In complete contrast to the self-discipline required in Zen Buddhism, the Pure Land sect teaches that self-discipline has nothing to do with salvation. Rather, people must have a strong faith in Amida Buddha, which they demonstrate by single-mindedly praying *Namu Amidabutsu*.

In one sense, this practice of invoking the name of a saint or holy spirit is not unlike the Christian teaching that people should seek salvation by invoking the name of Jesus Christ or the Virgin Mary. Christianity, however, also offers guidance to its adherents with regard to various ways of acting and behaving. This unity of faith and deeds to bring about salvation is what makes Christianity different from the absolute 'other-power' approach of Pure Land Buddhism.

If Zen Buddhism is considered a religion of practice, Pure Land Buddhism is a religion of faith. In Christianity, faith comes first and is followed by practice.

Just as many followers drifted away from Zen Buddhism, due largely to its severe austerity and discipline, the popularity of Pure Land Buddhism also waned. So long as respected holy priests at the high level of Hônen and Shinran were alive, people could see their enlightened ways of living on a daily basis, through their every deed. As they followed the examples of these holy leaders, their conduct naturally improved and they continued to chant the *Nembutsu* prayer with peace of mind. Thus, the Pure Land teachings achieved remarkable results. But as time went on and some of the sect's leaders failed to measure up to the standards of their predecessors, the 'easy path' of the Pure Land teachings became a shortcoming rather than a strength. People came to believe that in order to be saved, they need only recite the *Nembutsu* prayer, without making any daily efforts to cleanse their misguided ways. This kind of erroneous belief completely defiled the teachings of the sect's early leaders like Hônen and Shinran.

It was during this time that Nichiren Shônin appeared, and promoted a teaching based on wholehearted devotion to the *Hokekyô*, or Lotus Sutra. He vigorously condemned Zen Buddhism as a teaching of the devil, and warned that practitioners of invocations like the *Nembutsu* would fall into a bottomless hell.

If we ask whether the Lotus Sutra represents a self-power or other-power approach to enlightenment, it is absolute power itself. The Lotus Sutra described the manifestation of the Buddha purely and simply, in the image of the Holy Buddha itself. Its essence can be summed up in the words: *My body is the true body that cannot be burnt by fire nor drowned by water.* In other words, the true body of a human being is something that is not only immune to the effects of fire and water, but is also completely free. Thus, the Lotus Sutra is a teaching of absolute power.

However, for physical human beings living a physical life in this world, it is not only out of the question to manifest the absolute power of the true self without training of any kind, but it is also out of the question to gain knowledge of our true reality, which is the embodiment of absolute power. In zealous efforts to attain unity with the absolute power of the ultimate reality (Buddha), monks of both the Tendai and Zen sects engaged in training so austere that it almost seemed to shave away at their flesh. They endeavored to acquire true insight either through scholarship and philosophy, or through deep reflection in seated meditation. Essentially, they strived to attain their goal through power drawn from within themselves.

The adherents of the Nichiren sect, meanwhile, focused on manifesting the absolute power of the Lotus Sutra in this world through the recitation of either the seven-syllable prayer *Namu Myô Hôrengekyô* or the five-syllable variation, *Myô Hôrengekyô* (without *Namu*). Nichiren advocated the practice of manifesting absolute power through 'other-power' methods, centered around the recitation of these prayers. He believed that the act of reciting these prayers would bring about the manifestation of absolute power (the power of Buddha) in this world and wipe out all evil. With this firm belief, Nichiren staked his life on his teaching in order to demonstrate the benefits of Buddha in this world. In other words, he taught people of the benefits to be gained in this world through the observance of Buddhist teachings.

The Jôdo sect, on the other hand, placed emphasis on the Western Pure Land, or the idea of salvation in the next world. It provided its followers with peace of mind in this world through a sense of security that they had boarded 'Amida's prayer ship,' meaning that their salvation after death was guaranteed. There is no doubt that these two teachings, though their forms and methods may be different, aimed to guide people to attain Buddhahood through other-power. However, Nichiren sought mainly to save his society and the country as a whole through the recitation of prayers, and taught that people uplift themselves through this practice. Pure Land Buddhism started with the recitation of prayers as a means of self-salvation, and the belief developed that this practice would naturally rescue others as well, bringing them on board Amida's prayer ship and taking them to the blissful Pure Land.

Calling upon the Three Treasures

Although Zen Buddhism appears to be wholly grounded in absolute self-power, the chapter of *Dôshin* in the *Shôbôgenzô* by Dôgen Zenji states:

Whether asleep or awake, we should respectfully keep in mind the great spiritual benefits of the Three Treasures, and, whether asleep or awake, we should respectfully call upon the Three Treasures. For instance, during the interval between abandoning this life and not yet taking up the next life, there is what we call 'the intermediate existence'... At such a time, we should diligently apply our mind and respectfully call upon

*the Three Treasures, mindfully and ceaselessly reciting: 'I take
refuge in the Buddha (the awakened one), I take refuge in the
Dharma (the teaching), I take refuge in the Sangha (the com-
munity)'... Also, when this life of ours is coming to an end,
our two eyes may suddenly become dark. At such a time, knowing that the end of our life has come, we should strive to recite
the Refuges: "I take refuge in the Buddha..." and so forth...
After darkness has come before our eyes, we should, right off,
strive to recite the Three Refuges, not shirking from this even
during our entering the intermediate world or our next birth.
In this way, we should thoroughly expend life after life and, in
age after age, reverently recite Them.*[16]

We can see from this passage that, like Hônen and
Shinran of the Pure Land sect, Dôgen, too, was engaged
in the recitation of holy words and phrases. We can only
conclude that even Dôgen sought to attain Buddhahood
through other-power.

Even Dôgen, who is considered to be the most well-
known proponent of self-power training, used the other-
power method of reciting a holy prayer or mantra. He did
this along with the practice of Zen meditation, whose purpose is to manifest the internal image of Buddha through
self-power. Therefore, it can be said that there is no pure
self-power method in the world of religion. Zen Buddhism does, however, adopt an established form of seated
meditation to develop one's true mind (the merciful heart
of Buddha). During meditation followers are encouraged
to seek to overcome the various illusory thoughts, feelings, and desires that derive from their physical being. At

the same time, the religious leaders give strict, detailed guidance so that people do not become overwhelmed by these illusory thoughts.

The purpose of all these methods is to guide people to manifest Buddha (one's true mind or true body) through their own efforts and disciplined training. However, even in times when people did not have to worry too much about clothing, food, or making a living, these methods were unbearably difficult to follow for ordinary people whose souls were not yet elevated to higher realms. As a result, there were very few who gained spiritual peace and enlightenment through these methods.

In this day and age when people need to spend the majority of their waking hours earning a living and providing for the daily needs of their families and themselves, the idea of attaining spiritual peace and enlightenment by following the rigorous training of Zen Buddhism seems next to impossible. This is why, in recent times, the overwhelming majority of people have been drawn to a *tariki*, or other-power, approach to salvation, and the sects that follow this approach are flourishing.

Human beings and the divine are a single beam of light

The Jôdo (Pure Land) and Jôdo Shinshû (True Pure Land) sects are both established sects of Buddhism based on 'other-power,' and various Nichiren sects developed encompassing both established and new sects. The new sects of Ômotokyô and Tenrikyô have very large followings, and Christianity, as a global religion, also has an enormous number of adherents. All of these religions guide people to seek salvation through other-power—a power beyond the power of the self—or, they guide people to envision an absolute divine being with the power to draw out their inner truth (the heart of Buddha) within. As a means to do this, people are taught to engage in reciting prayers, mantras, or other incantations.

However, the creeds that seem to account for the majority of today's religions, while they may appear to subscribe to other-power methods, are not like the genuine other-power teachings that were seen in the time of Hônen and Shinran. They may teach that human beings are lives branching out from the absolute divine being, and that our life is sustained by divine power. Or, as in the case of the Lotus Sutra, they may teach that a human being is God itself, and that the phenomena appearing in this world as evil or misfortune are nothing but manifestations of illusory thoughts, and are not true realities. However, they do not view God and human beings as being in a single continuum as a stream of light, but instead see the two as being far apart from each other.

Without a fundamental belief that God and human beings form an unbroken stream of light which together constitute a single entity, there can be no absolute salvation. And there can be no absolute other-power where we entrust our entire self to the divine.

In other words, as long as we maintain the notion that negative karma and negative causes and effects originate in the human mind and undeniably exist in the human world in opposition to the divine will, we cannot expect to be uplifted by a divine power unless we wholeheartedly offer prayers to that divine power while curbing our karmic thoughts and actions.

To put it another way, for as long as we recognize evil and adversity in the thoughts and actions of ourselves and others, we will never be able to reach the absolute world of the Lotus Sutra—the world of absolute freedom, truth, and beauty.

The teachings of both Hônen and Shinran also emphasized this point, explaining that, irrespective of a physical person's thoughts and deeds, that person could reach the Pure Land of Amida Buddha through ardent recitation of the *Nembutsu* prayer. Nowhere in their teachings did it say that unless an errant person made amends for past deeds, that person could not be saved by Amida Buddha, no matter how fervent the person's prayers might be. This was because the founders of Pure Land Buddhism knew that every human being was a Buddha. They taught that, while human beings are originally Buddhas, before they became aware of this they first became absorbed in mistaken ideas that caused them to unknowingly distance themselves from Buddha. While adhering to a world of mistaken ideas deriving from past karmic thoughts, people would never find Buddha no matter how eagerly they searched, because waves of past mistaken thoughts would continually surge forth and prevent them from doing so. Instead, they advised people to sever their attachment to the past and persevere in devoted prayer to Amida Buddha. Rather than going back to their past karmic selves, they said, people should press forward with steadfast recitation of the *Nembutsu*. Then, their thoughts would no longer be pulled back by karmic waves from the past, and they could be united with Buddha and return to their original self—a state of perfect freedom and salvation.

This, essentially, was the core of Hônen's and Shinran's teachings. Without this fundamental teaching, the founders of Pure Land Buddhism would not have been able to declare that no matter how wicked a person might have been in the past, that person could still be saved through devoted prayer to Amida Buddha.

Absolute power through pure other-power

The majority of religious leaders today, while promoting total entrustment of the self to a divine power, make constant references to the evil minds of their adherents. They try to compel believers to practice the teachings while continually judging and condemning their behavior.

If we decide to follow a self-power approach, we must meditate and contemplate spiritual truth exhaustively, as Dôgen and Hakuin did, to develop our true mind, even with some strict ascetic training. If this is out of the question, it behooves us to move forward on the path of absolute other-power, as Hônen and Shinran did. Otherwise, we will never find everlasting salvation or manifest the Pure Land in this earthly world.

At a time like today when the fate of the earth is at stake, a superficial religious concept serves no purpose. I do not believe the way of absolute self-power is an option for me, nor do I believe it is for people in general and, therefore, I have been steadfastly pursuing the path of absolute other-power. As a result, I have been encouraging people to continually pray for world peace, and to allow their thoughts to be purified within the bright vibrations of the prayer.

God is love itself, and the true dwelling place of human beings is within God. It is only that our past mistaken thoughts have been obstructing the divine light from directly flowing into this physical world. Fortunately, we have guardian divinities and guardian spirits, whose role is to constantly watch over us physical beings. They protect us without interruption with the light of divine love. I know this clearly through my own daily experiences, and therefore I can state it with absolute assurance.

Although we human beings are receiving this spiritual guidance and protection, we continue to repeat the same mistakes over and over again. This is because the protective power of our guardian spirits is a power that does not come into contact with our five senses, while the power of karmic thoughts is directly connected with our five senses. As physical beings, our thoughts are naturally attracted to a power that is linked with the five senses, and so we have a tendency to stray from the light of our guardian divinities and spirits, significantly diminishing the effects of their precious power.

Therefore, it is my intention to bring the thoughts of human beings closer to our guardian divinities and spirits, and I have been urging people to tirelessly repeat in their minds words of appreciation for the divine and spiritual protectors that watch over them.

At the same time, it is important for us to remember that any evil or adversity (including illness) arising from karmic thoughts did not exist originally in human beings, and is bound to fade away. I therefore say to people, do not be taken in by the evil, adversity, or mistaken ideas that may appear before you temporarily. Instead, convert your thoughts of clinging to these negative events into thoughts of gratitude for the presence of your guardian divinities and spirits. Then, take this one step further by elevating your mind from thoughts of your own salvation to prayer for world peace.

If you see yourself or another person as 'bad,' that is not a true form, but is a form that is fading away. All you need to do is turn your thoughts to prayer for world peace and carry on with your daily life. This method, which starts with an other-power practice and changes to absolute power, is the best spiritual method that I know to manifest the paradise of the Pure Land, or heaven, on earth. The divine mind has conveyed this to humanity through my physical entity.

DEVELOPING
YOUR SPIRITUALITY

To be truly free from all trouble and pain, human beings must inevitably develop what is called their 'spirituality.' There is no other way for human beings to attain true peace. No matter how much people may talk about peace and clamor for the establishment of a unified world, their cries will have no effect if they have not developed their spirituality. That kind of talk will never bring about world peace, nor will it hasten the birth of a unified world.

I say this because, as human beings, our original nature is our spiritual being, and not our physical body. Those who think that we are simply physical bodies and nothing more live in a way that makes it impossible for them to walk along their own true path.

Why, then, does our true nature consist of our spirituality, and not our physical body? In Japanese, the word for spirit is *rei* (霊), and the word *rei* can also mean 'zero'. Both 'spirit' and 'zero' refer to the aspect of something before it appears on the surface as 'one.' If we say that what appears on the surface as 'one,' 'two,' or 'three' belongs to the phenomenal, or tangible, world (in other words, material manifestations including the physical body) then we can think of that which is not perceived by the five senses, as 'spirit,' or 'zero.'

If this is so, then which category does life belong to? Life itself cannot be seen, heard, or otherwise perceived by the five senses. Life can only by grasped in terms of its activity.

The heart, lungs, stomach, and intestines continue to function while life is active in the physical body. But once life leaves the physical body, our organs immediately stop their work. They still exist in the physical body, and the body itself also exists, but it ceases to perform any function.

This means that without the thing called 'life,' which is not seen by the eyes or felt by the hands, the existence of the physical body and internal organs, which can be seen by the eyes and felt by the hands, turns into something completely inactive and meaningless.

When we think along these lines, it follows that the material objects that are tangible to our five senses are like tools, or containers, belonging to a particular time and place, and that the thing called 'life' is the real essence of a human being.

This plain truth is something that no one is able to deny. Even so, the vast majority of people today consider only the material aspects of a human being—those that are perceived by the five senses. They think of 'life,' which animates and controls the physical body, as if it were merely an internal existence within the physical body, and that the physical body itself is the main thing. This idea is humankind's greatest error. For as long as humanity keeps basing all its thoughts and actions on this idea, it will be forever unable to manifest its own intrinsic truth.

Until people start thinking about this world and human society on the basis of the thing called 'life,' not only will humankind go on living from moment to moment and place to place in mutual selfishness, and not only will we be unable to realize our ideal of making evolutionary progress, but we will continue moving closer and closer to the abyss of destruction.

The source of human faculties

If you take the standpoint that human life exists only as an attribute of each individual physical body, then you will naturally think that when a person's physical body perishes, that person has vanished forever and become nonexistent. You will think that the person's way of living and way of thinking have simply disappeared. But in truth, this is not the case.

It often happens that a person's will is carried on by others who try to fulfill the work that he or she began. Naturally, if a person's work concerns the greater good, a larger portion of it is likely to be carried on by other people. What this suggests is that the essence of the thing called 'life,' which activates the physical body, is something that wishes to be of help to other lives. In other words, though life appears to be contained within separate physical embodiments, it actually works in connection with other lives.

Thus, it naturally follows that the will of someone who lived too individualistically is seldom carried on by others. On the other hand, the sort of work and ideals that come from humanitarian or socially-oriented motives are taken up by large numbers of people.

This is consistent with the view that while life works within each physical body, it is at the same time connected with many other lives. The sum total of all those lives can be called the Great Life. The Great Life functions in each physical body as a small, individual life. Without showing itself, it activates the various physical organs and serves as the motive power for our ability to think. Could this life-power be something material, something devoid of wisdom or perception? We can readily answer *No*. Why do we answer *No*? It is because as human beings, we are able to function thanks to the power of life, and this functioning is always rooted in wisdom and perception. Consequently, we can only conclude that wisdom and perception are contained within life itself.

In terms of its function, life is clearly discernible through the workings of the various physical organs. However, the substance of life is not something we can see or touch. It is a thing without shape—a spirit. The composite of all individual lives, known as the Great Life, can therefore be called the 'Great Spirit.'

To explain it systematically, the source of each life

radiates from the Great Spirit. Each individual life is thus a division, or branch, of the Great Spirit. Through these divisions, or branches, the Great Spirit acts directly in this world. Each human being is one of the individual spirits branching out from the Great Spirit.

According to this principle, it is very clear that all human faculties come from the Great Spirit. Yet, for people who are convinced that a human being is nothing more than a material body, this simple truth is very difficult to understand.

The law of karma

What prevents people from understanding this principle is karmic thinking (we could also call it karma, darkness, or illusion). The further people distance themselves from their spirituality, the more extensive this karma (disorder and corruption) becomes. However, since karmic thoughts and activities are not part of our original nature, once they accumulate to a certain point they have to extinguish themselves. They collide with other karmic vibrations, crumble apart, and vanish. This disintegration process causes various misfortunes, such as strife and warfare, injury and illness, failure, and natural disasters, to appear.

When they do not know this principle, human beings try to pull back to themselves the karma that is being manifested and extinguished in the form of various misfortunes. They do this by emitting karmic thoughts such as dissatisfaction, fear, anger, jealousy, and resentment.

The reason why these thoughts have the effect of pulling back the karma that is meant to vanish is that they are composed of the same kinds of vibrations. The disintegrating karma is also made up of thoughts of uneasiness, discontent, fear, anger, and so on. When people's newly generated thoughts have the same wavelength as that of the disappearing karma, they intermingle with those karmic waves and bond together with them. As a result, though the earlier karma has begun to fade away, it cannot vanish entirely, and becomes lodged within the karmic waves that were generated later.

The Great Spirit (the divine mind, or God) is, indeed, the origin of all power. It is harmony itself. It is what links all things together. In order for great harmony to take shape and manifest in this world, humanity's karmic thoughts must crumble and vanish away. When this occurs, our role is to direct our attention to the divine principles that are about to manifest themselves. Instead, however, people are focusing their attention on the karmic side, giving rise to new thoughts of anxiety, discontent, fear, resentment, and so on.

Worrisome and unsatisfactory conditions come back to people who have thoughts of uneasiness and discontent. Resentment comes back to people who resent others. All the things that a person sends out come back to that person. This is the law of karma. This thing called karma is not something that appeared because there is no God. Karma is also moved, indirectly, by divine power. It disintegrates and vanishes at the time when the divine will deems it to be unnecessary.

The relationship between God and the movements of karma

Now, this is a very important point. If the movements of karma were to be independent of any relationship with God, then God and karma would be relative to each other. They would stand in opposition to one another and fight against one another. Ancient religious leaders made God and Satan (karma) into two entities, and taught that Satan (karma) is an independent existence. Indeed, when we look at the condition of the world today, we might be inclined to think that way. Yet if this were the case, the struggles of this world would have to continue forever. People would simply want to follow the side with the greater chances of winning. Under these circumstances, we would not be able to firmly assert that God is the one and only, absolute existence.

If it were not possible to freely extinguish any karma solely through the divine will, then the principle of God's absoluteness, infiniteness, and omnipotence would not hold true. Human beings would not be able to find peace and security in knowing that they are children of God.

It is because we human beings are children of God, and are spiritual in nature, that we have the means of overcoming karma. When we clearly bring out our spirituality, letting life express itself within us just as it is, a way of living based solely on our divine nature will open up for us, and all darkness will eventually vanish away. If this were not a true principle, spiritual faith would have no purpose.

Why was karma born?

What does it mean to say that karma moves when divine power acts upon it indirectly? To give a broad outline, karma itself was born when divine life began to work on earth in the form of physical human beings. Prior to the birth of physical human beings in the earthly world, karma did not exist there.

Just as there is no darkness in a world made up entirely of light, without the existence of light, darkness does not recognize itself as darkness. But once light begins to penetrate the darkness, the distinction between light and darkness becomes clear. Then, as the light advances, the figure of darkness is eliminated proportionately. Its form is chipped away and removed, bit by bit. If we say that God is light, then since the time when God's light began to work on earth as human life, the darkness, or backwardness, on earth has been gradually and proportionately undergoing development.

In order for the divine light rays to be put to work in the earthly world, it was essential for them to have material bodies made up of the same substance as the earthly world itself. This is how the existence of individual physical human beings came about. Since the physical human body is a material body, belonging to the earthly world, it has an earthly nature. Consequently, as the divine light keeps advancing in the earthly world, and its undeveloped condition undergoes development, various kinds of tremblings, shakings, and transformations occur. When physical human beings first experienced these tremblings and changes, they thought of them in the opposite sense. They mistakenly identified themselves with darkness instead of identifying themselves with light. They viewed the collapsing shapes of darkness as the collapsing shapes of themselves. They then emitted thoughts of unrest and fear. This way of thinking, which is removed from divine light, or from spirituality, is darkness. This is the cause of the birth of karma. In Christian terms, this would be called the 'original sin' of Adam and Eve.

In this way, humanity forgot its original identity. People forgot that they are divine light itself. They mistakenly thought that they were a product of darkness. They mistakenly thought of themselves as earthbound, physical existences. This is the major cause of what is referred to as 'sin.'

Knowing the oneness of life

If you think that a human being is merely a physical existence it is only natural for you to see yourself and others as being totally separate from one another. For as long as you think this way, you cannot see yourself and others as being different manifestations of one divine life that takes individual forms in order to reveal a variety of divine concepts and ideas here in the earthly world.

The only people who can say that human beings share one and the same life are people who believe in the existence of God. These words cannot be said by materially-minded people, or by people who think that a human being is simply flesh and bone. If a person knows that all human beings share the same life, how could that person be so keen on outranking others and securing happiness for themselves alone, or for their own group or country, that they would go so far as to harm other human beings?

When I observe the way individuals and nations are living today, I cannot help being surprised at how few of them live with a view of the true oneness of life. It is unmistakably true that this occurs because earthly humanity has not clearly developed its spirituality. When we are aware of our own spirituality and the spirituality of others, and know that our physical body, like the physical bodies of others, is a container and a workplace for the spirit, there can be no reason for us to beat others down in order to protect our own body, or to be downtrodden by physical illness or misfortune.

For as long as humanity keeps on its present course, without trying to know that they are not flesh but spirit, and are beings whose natural purpose is to give expression to the ideas of God, they have no choice but to go on experiencing lifetime after lifetime in this karmic world, never finding relief and never seeing the light.

The way things are at present, the authority for day-to-day decision making is held by political figures and members of the higher echelons of society, who generally do not know of the connection between the divine—the Great Spirit and all-encompassing life—and human beings, who are individual spirits, or divine offspring. Unless this condition reverses itself completely, and the world begins to move forward under the guidance of people who clearly know the harmonious spirit of God, no policies—whether of threat, compromise, or peacemaking—will be able to rescue the population of earth.

How to develop your spirituality

What should you do, then, in order to develop your spirituality?

In a nutshell, the key is not to think of anything except divinity. Up to now, spiritual leaders have taught of God, but at the same time, behind these words they have often criticized the actions of their adherents, and have advised them to overcome karmic thinking with their own individual power. But I do not adopt this method. I recommend that people think only of divinity, from beginning to end, thoroughly and completely.

My method is to cast aside the various thoughts that come to mind of injuring yourself and others, recognizing those thoughts as vanishing traces of a past consciousness that are pushing themselves out onto the surface in order to fade away and disappear forever. As you do this, I also recommend that you continuously and intently call the name of God in your heart. To practice a teaching which makes people preoccupy themselves with every little detail of the karmic thoughts that appear is like putting the branch in place of the root, and it enslaves your mind to the karmic thoughts and actions of yourself and others, seriously retarding the development of your divine nature.

If they know that God is all of everything, why do spiritual leaders not ask their believers to think only of God? Why do they instead give teachings that stir up more and more karmic thinking, reinforcing and perpetuating the mistakes people made in the past with their physical consciousness?

To say such things as, "In your heart you are harboring this defect or that vice," or "human beings are born of sin," and so forth, may sound like very religious teachings. In reality, though, this is quite different from true religion.

True religion is what wakens the awareness that human beings come from God and are none other than light itself—none other than truth, goodness, and beauty. The teaching that human beings are 'born of sin' is something that refers to physical human beings, and it has nothing to do with our essential nature, which is our spirituality. Words like 'born of sin' are said in order to emphasize the helplessness of the physical self. They are not what we ought to say to people who are wholeheartedly trying to entrust themselves to God.

This is why I say that in order to guide people along the road to true deliverance, the most important thing is the development of their spirituality.

In olden times, people used to become monks or ascetics and seclude themselves in the mountains or meditate under waterfalls in order to develop their spirituality. However, we cannot thoroughly and continuously practice such disciplines if we also carry the responsibility of a spouse and family. Consequently, the general population can hardly be expected to engage in such practices, and thus they are not practical training methods for modern day society.

The first ones to take note of this were Hônen, Shinran,

and other advocates of the Pure Land school of teachings during Japan's Kamakura period. To wholeheartedly re-cite the *Nembutsu* (see chapter 3) was to think deeply and single-mindedly of God, and this was equivalent to put-ting all your effort into flinging all your thoughts and ac-tions into God. This method was an easy way for people to develop their spirituality without disrupting their normal daily life, and it allowed them to firmly connect them-selves with the divine world.

Among the people who misunderstand the develop-ment of spirituality, there seem to be some who simply think that spirituality means perceiving things that are outside the realm of our five senses. However, this is a very dangerous idea. What is meant by developed spiri-tuality is that a person's thoughts and actions can always reflect the mind of God, which is love, truth, goodness and beauty. It does not simply mean being able to sense things which the average person cannot.

This is a crucial point in the development of spiritual-ity. If you try to develop your spirituality for purposes of personal gain or short-term advantage, and if you are satisfied with being able to see, hear, feel, and do things which others cannot, feeling a sense of superiority over others, having this sort of attitude in your heart means that you are heading in an entirely different direction from the development of spirituality. I say this because when a person feels superior to others, or practices ascetic discipline for worldly benefits, that in itself means that he or she has already stepped outside the principle that hu-man beings are one unified, divine life.

Practically speaking, though, this self-centered way of thinking is a very difficult thing to get rid of, and it is how the vast majority of people continue to think and act. This is what makes the development of spirituality all the more necessary.

Prayer for world peace

Now more than ever, it is vitally necessary for all human beings to develop their spirituality and manifest their true identity here in this earthly world. The true identity of a human being is, in other words, the image of a child of God.

For this reason, spiritual leaders who simply preach religious dogmas or offer worldly gains have become unnecessary in this day and age. What we need are spiritual leaders who will teach the true development of spirituality in a way that the average person will be able to put into practice.

Spiritually awakened leaders are also needed, to explain how nations and humanity as a whole can call forth and give expression to their inherent divine nature. Among these awakened individuals there might be religious leaders, scientists, or statesmen. Whatever their field might be, I do not think they can effectively carry out their work unless, from the start, they understand that the spiritual development of all humanity is the fundamental goal to be aimed for.

For this reason, I have been given the mission, first of all, of assisting the general population in developing their spirituality. Consequently, I have put into modern language the Easy Path that has continued since the days of Hônen and Shinran, and I have been letting many people know about it. It is a method based in prayer for world peace.

When we mention the development of spirituality, people who know even a little about spiritual methods might immediately envision disciplines such as sitting meditation, meditating under waterfalls, fasting, and so on. Although these disciplines are one way of developing spirituality, it must be noted that they are not the most suitable training methods for contemporary times.

As I have already mentioned, I believe that the spiritual training method of today is the path opened up by the two great saints Hônen and Shinran, and also in the teachings of Jesus Christ. I say this because, in the present age, with its complex lifestyles and social systems, austere training methods are totally unattainable for everyone except certain special people.

If you understand that God is always at work within human beings, then you have already developed your spirituality. But if you can advance even one step further, and understand that the divine world is a perfectly harmonious world of brilliant glory, free from any unharmonious things such as evil, unhappiness or illness, and if you know that the unharmonious conditions that now appear in our surroundings are the disappearing images of our own thoughts and actions, generated during a past consciousness, when we separated ourselves from God, and if you can always keep thoughts of gratitude in your mind, deeply appreciating the fact that all negativities are disappearing, it means you have already become someone whose divine nature is fully developed. Your true identity as a child of God is being manifested in this world. You unknowingly brighten the people around you, and you are naturally able to perform actions which help many people to develop their own spirituality.

The method that enables people to become this kind of person within their normal daily life, with no need for hard discipline or strain, is the method of prayer for world peace.

World peace is the condition where divinity manifests itself through each and every human being. World peace means that the divine mind—the ideas of God—are realized in this world with no element of distortion. This is why, when you think of praying for world peace, you are already on the road to spiritual development. And the great value of this prayer, as a prayer for modern times, is that it is both a prayer for individual spiritual development and also a prayer for human society as a whole.

NOTES

1. *Mu* (無), a teaching of Lao Tsu and also of Buddhism, might be described as freedom from the ego. *Mu* literally means 'none' or 'without.'

2. *Kuu* (空) could be translated as 'emptiness' or 'nothingness.' Masahisa Goi explains: *Kuu* is not a nihilistic or negative condition. It contains nothing, yet everything. It is the life of God, just as it is, living vibrantly.

3. The work of divine and spiritual protectors (also called guardian divinities and spirits) is described in Masahisa Goi's book *God and Man* (Byakko Press, 2005). It is also discussed in chapter 4 of this book.

4. *One Who Unites Heaven and Earth* (Byakko Press, 2005) is the autobiography of Masahisa Goi's early life.

5. The term used in the original is *kami kara wakerareta* (神から分けられた), which means 'issuing from God' or 'branching out from God.'

6. In his other writings and talks the author has mentioned that materialistic thinking is the source of the struggles and anxieties of the present day world, and is leading the world toward its destruction.

7. Hônen lived in Japan from 1130 to 1212.

8. *Shôdômon* (聖道門) was a way of striving for awakening by means of 'self-effort' rather than 'reliance on God.'

9. Amitâbha in Sanskrit. Amida Buddha is sometimes called 'the Buddha of Infinite Light.'

10. A bodhisattva is someone who wishes to awaken so as to work for the deliverance of others. Hôzô Bodhisattva is also known as Dharmakara.

11. This recitation is known in Japanese as the *Nembutsu* (念仏). The *Nembutsu* is a method for thinking only of God.

12. Shinran (1173-1262) was a priest and a disciple of Hônen who carried on the teachings of the Pure Land sect of Buddhism.

13. Nichiren (1222-1282) was the founder of the Nichiren sect of Buddhism.

14. Although Sakyamuni Buddha was no longer living on Earth at the time when the *Nembutsu* came into being,

the author maintains that during his lifetime, Sakyamuni advocated recitation methods similar to the *Nembutsu*.

15. In Japanese, sitting meditation is called *zazen* (座禅).

16. Excerpted from Chapter 94 of *Shôbôgenzô: The Treasure House of the Eye of the True Teaching* by Eihei Dôgen, Translated by Rev. Hubert Nearman, O.B.C., Shasta Abbey Press, 2007. http://www.browardzen.com/docs/Shobogenzo.pdf

ABOUT THE AUTHOR

 Born in Tokyo, Japan, on November 22, 1916, Masahisa Goi was a poet, philosopher, writer, and singer. Though he aimed at a career in music, he found himself spontaneously drawn to the realms of philosophy and spiritual guidance. At the age of 33 he attained oneness with his divine self. From that time on, he endeavored to reach out to people by holding informal talks, where anyone was invited to participate and ask questions. He enjoyed this direct contact with people, and provided many with spiritual guidance toward the attainment of inner peace.

Mr. Goi authored more than 60 books and volumes of poetry, including *God and Man* (his first and most fundamental work), *One Who Unites Heaven and Earth* (an autobiography of his early life), *The Spirit of Lao Tsu*, *Essays on the Bible*, *How to Develop Your Spirituality*, and *Catch the Light*, to name a few. Translations of many of his works are in progress.

Based on the universal prayer *May Peace Prevail on Earth* which he advocated, Masahisa Goi founded a worldwide movement of world peace through prayer, transcending religious, ethnic, and political boundaries. Before departing from this world in 1980, he named Mrs. Masami Saionji, his adopted daughter, as his successor and leader of the world peace prayer movement that he initiated.

CPSIA information can be obtained at www.ICGtesting.com
Printed in the USA
LVOW10s2008101214

418176LV00033B/2247/P